THE CAM COACH

by

Mark Shields & Simon Martin

Grosvenor House
Publishing Limited

This book is published by
Grosvenor House Publishing Ltd
28-30 High Street, Guildford, Surrey, GU1 3EL.
www.grosvenorhousepublishing.co.uk

A CIP record for this book
is available from the British Library

ISBN 978-1-78148-129-5

Contents

The Birth of the CAM Coach

Many people would have said I had it all. A house on the hill, sea view, boat in the harbour, great job, a wonderful wife and family and to top it all I lived on the Channel Islands.

If that doesn't top it all I had a six figure salary, riches beyond my wildest dreams - or so I thought.

I was the head of a well-known bank and we were achieving great results, I had a great team of people I worked with and life was good; how much better does it get than that? I had recently been awarded the bank's prestigious manager of the year "best of the best" award, which had been a great achievement and honour - and a complete surprise at the time it is fair to add.

My wife had a job at the local heritage trust, my daughter was at the local nursery and my son had just been born. Nothing could have been better.

I just had one big problem.

I was bored.

No, really bored.

Really, really bored. So bored I felt guilty every day I went in that I didn't deserve the money I was being paid.

I'd worked out I had somebody in my team that did everything for me, even writing the bank's cheques for me to sign and updating the sales results boards on my office wall while I sat there and watched.

What was there left for me to do?

I was 38 years old and had achieved everything I had set out to achieve. I had a great PA and a second personal assistant that did everything for me from booking my flights to taking notes at meetings I attended, and to top it all, my sector of the bank was achieving every target we had been given, several times over. I needed a change, a challenge, something that would in some bizarre way allow me to once again face the challenge and excitement I had got in the past when climbing that corporate ladder.

I cast my mind back to the beginning, some 22 years before.

There I was at 16 with my mother in British Home Stores, buying my first business suit. It was grey and I also got a maroon stripy tie; my mother loved it, I hated it, especially that maroon tie. I hoped none of my friends could see me. It was my first job interview with one of the major 5 high street banks. I felt confident, I had my five "O" levels, been told I was good at admin, so what could go wrong? After all, I was only going for the job of filing clerk.

Somewhere along the way the new grey suit, or it could have been the tie, let me down and I was rejected. A young lady in a very smart red jacket got the job. She certainly didn't get her jacket from BHS. They thought she had more to offer; I am sure she did. I was devastated, but always remembered my first experience of not getting that job. It wouldn't happen again, especially not with that bank, and I was relentless about one day putting the record straight.

That bank remained in my sights for years to come. Ironic then that I ended up running a large sector of that same bank 22 years later, still with the same 5 "O" levels, but they didn't seem to matter anymore -nobody seemed to care.

Back to present day: the grey suit, girl in the red jacket and stripy maroon tie seemingly a long way off. It was one of those lazy summer days in the Channel Islands. I was in the kitchen when my wife Karen appeared around the fridge door in a state of both panic and delight. "It's him again, that guy on tv who can do everything, the life guru!"

I knew who she meant straight away and the fact he was blessed with film-star looks definitely held Karen's interest.

"Everything", I repeated to myself. I cautiously entered the lounge and there he was, the man that supposedly does everything, film star looks and all. He was in full flow, helping a very frightened looking groom get over his wedding nerves. The more I watched the more intrigued I became.

I was watching a programme called The Life Guru; the star of the show was somebody called Alistair Horscroft, a life coach and NLP Practitioner who had been plucked from obscurity to star as the show's expert and host.

My earliest memories of the world of Complementary and Alternative Medicine was watching Alistair that day being interviewed on the tv, talking about another patient he had cured, another challenge he had overcome, and another miracle he seemed to have performed. I remember he looked as amazed as everyone when changing yet another mere mortal's life forever, and he simply stated that the power of the mind was incredible and anything was possible. Or words to that effect.

Here was a man who was incredibly successful, often someone's last resort, and he seemed to offer the miracle cure time and time again. He had his own tv show to prove it. The Life Guru was featured every week, curing all sorts of people, from all sorts of problems and phobias.

I vividly remember watching the great man that day, and wondering exactly how he did the amazing things he did, how he had so much knowledge about the mind, nutrition and his whole holistic approach to mind and body fitness. That was it. I had to meet this guy and find out how he did the wonderful things he did. He lived in Sydney, but just happened to be flying to London to run an NLP, Hypnosis, and Coaching course at the end of the year.

Seven years later and the rest is history. Alistair and I remain firm friends to this day. The Life Practice was born and our business has enjoyed unprecedented success, with us opening a nutritional arm to our practice as well as business coaching and mentoring thousands of Complementary and Alternative Medical practitioners all over the world.

In addition we have our own certified and accredited training courses designed specifically to provide a way for our students to obtain the skills, knowledge and confidence required to become wellbeing practitioners themselves and forge an exciting future for themselves in the CAM industry

With products in Waterstones, a regular slot on BBC radio as their resident life coach and a growing team of Associates opening Life Practice Offices all over the UK, life is fantastic and wonderfully challenging and unrecognisable from my days at the bank.

As a business we have always featured heavily in the media and it was in this way, quite by chance, I met my writing partner Simon Martin.

Most of you will know Simon as the editor of the fabulous CAM magazine, but few will know he is also trained as an NLP and life coach and has used his knowledge of NLP, nutrition and other CAM modalities to become a world champion masters athlete.

Simon and I hit it off immediately and we agreed I should write a monthly column for CAM, the theme of which should be helping fellow practitioners achieve success in their respective CAM businesses. Practitioner Proficiencies was born and is still running to this day.

Both Simon and I shared a concern of how difficult it appeared to be to run a successful CAM practice. We jointly researched the results and found to our dismay that around 65% of CAM students finishing their courses, even degree courses, didn't make it into practice and of those that did many failed in the first 12 months.

The frightening comparison, if this isn't scary enough, is between a complementary practitioner's first year in business compared to a business start-up in a different industry: 20% more CAM practices fail in their first year than in other business start-up areas.

We felt we had a duty of care to try and do something about this, as we both believe totally in the importance of complementary and alternative medicine. So the CAM Coach concept was born and the book was to follow.

Within the context of the book you will notice we may refer to your particular therapeutic discipline in an obscure way or perhaps even not at all. Let me reassure you this book is aimed at and will add value to every type of CAM business in existence today. The key principles are the same for us all. So whether you are a Nutritional Therapist, Medical Herbalist/ Phytotherapist, Hypnotherapist, Personal Trainer, Energy worker, Psychotherapist, Naturopath, Acupuncturist, Chiropractor, Osteopath or whatever, we refer to you all as CAM practitioners, therapists, and coaches.

Simon defers to me as the business and financial brain, as he is self-admittedly "rubbish" in those areas. I've held nothing back in the book. I'm sharing all of my secrets on how to set up and run a successful alternative medicine business. These are secrets, strategies and key principles that have actually been used successfully in the field over the last 7 years with thousands of clients, practitioners and students and have proved to work. Not only work, but work well and deliver outstanding results.

By reading this book and adopting the principles in it you are what we call in the NLP world, modelling success. Copying and adhering to key principles that actually work. Not subjective theory that someone somewhere thinks is a good idea, but proven business strategies that not only work, but work well.

It's not practice that ensures good performance, but perfect practice that ensures perfect performance - "the difference that makes the difference", as I call it.

I would strongly urge you to read this book with an open mind. Don't be afraid of trying something new - it's quite normal to be nervous; we are all afraid of what we don't know.

What we can say for sure is that if you always do what you've always done, you'll always get what you've always got.

Wishing you enlightening reading, in the hope that the knowledge contained within these pages will take you and your business to a new and exciting level of personal success for you and your clients.

Mark Shields, 2012

About the authors

Mark Shields is the founder of The Life Practice Group. He is nationally respected as a successful Life and Business Coach, Media Expert, Author and Motivational Speaker, appearing regularly on tv and radio.

He has worked successfully with thousands of clients from the entertainment industry, including tv presenters, as well as with world champion sportsmen, senior business leaders, famous musicians and senior government politicians.

Simon Martin is the editor of CAM magazine and a journalist who has been writing and researching alternative medicine and natural health for more than 30 years.

A former editor of Here's Health and the Journal of Alternative Medicine, he is a graduate of the University of Westminster's pioneering BSc (Hons) Health Sciences degree programme.

Part 1: Setting up your Successful Practice

Chapter 1: Starting Out

To paraphrase one of the most famous lines in movie history, mouthed by Clint "Dirty Harry" Eastwood: "We know what you're thinking".

This is all the boring stuff, right? Setting up as a business, dealing with insurance, accounting, banking...what's this got to do with you as a CAM practitioner, whose calling is to help people?

Well, there are people who actually enjoy these nuts and bolts. Mark is one of them. Uniquely, for someone with his business background, he's also very good at communicating what needs to be done – and finding ways that make dealing with all this actually fun. As Julie Thompson Crawley writes about one of the essential "boring" tasks Mark set her: "The first job in hand was to write down the goals for the business. I have never done this before and actually thought it was a complete waste of time! Boy was I wrong; this is the most amazing thing to do ever...it really gets your head into the right place and I certainly needed all the help I could get. Do this exercise. I hope it inspires you as much as it did me and still does." Read more from her in "A New Practitioner's Tale" in this chapter.

And really, we do know what (most of you) are thinking. Simon, being the polar opposite to Mark when it comes to hard business skills, knows that this is the part of the book you are most likely to skip over. It's the part HE wanted to skip over! So by all means check out all the inspiring case histories we've included if you need that bit of extra motivation for the nuts and bolts. But be aware that all the successful practitioners we've included have their practices on firm business foundations. They've organised things that way because it has made them better able to help many more people than they would otherwise reach.

But hey, why listen to us? You haven't got to know us yet. So maybe these words from Jayney Goddard, president of the Complementary Medical Association, will help. The CMA was set up in 1995 and is one of the UK's best-known professional bodies, representing more than 15,000 practitioners and 100 colleges. Jayney says:

"I've trained thousands of practitioners over the last few years in business development and hear time and again that viewing themselves and their practices as commercial entities is often a hard leap for practitioners to make - as they are inherently altruistic beings. However, the cold hard reality is that if complementary medicine, as a whole, is to survive and thrive under the well-orchestrated, well-funded attacks that we have seen - we, as practitioners, have to 'up the ante' and re-frame ourselves as business professionals.

"I believe in the ripple effect, such that if a practitioner is successful and profitable, they will be able to invest in their business, thus making their work more available to clients. This, in turn, creates a positive feedback loop throughout their immediate social circle, eventually promoting complementary medicine further into society - making it more accessible, better understood and more acceptable."

According to the CMA president, this more business-orientated outlook is becoming a major trend among practitioners. If you are going to survive long enough to put your training and personal vision into action, getting these nuts and bolts right is essential. We'll make it as fun as we can – just remember that our aim is to give you everything you need to succeed. So stay with the programme!

As Jayney added: "The most profound change that I have personally noticed in our profession over the last ten years is the growing awareness among practitioners of the need to 'professionalise' their practice work. Practitioners now realise the importance of maintaining a profitable practice which thrives - as a 'business'."

• A New Practitioner's Tale

Let me tell you about the adventure of setting up my own practice...

First of all get rid of any nagging doubts: "What if I don't succeed?" "What if I can't make enough money?" Or "I'm not good enough". I wasted 2 years with all of this self-doubt, working long hours for someone else and not making any money. Finally the penny dropped - why are you wasting all this time? Come on, get there, get this business started! So I handed in my notice and got a part-time job to keep me going

The adventure began...for the first time in years I felt excited about getting up in the morning. Most of the nagging thoughts had gone, although a few still floated in and out but hey, you've got to be in it to win it!

The first job in hand was to write down the goals for the business. I had never done this before and actually thought it was a complete waste of time! Boy was I wrong; this is the most amazing thing to do ever...it really gets your head into the right place and I certainly needed all the help I could get. Do this exercise. I hope it inspires you as much as it did me and still does. I look at my goal book regularly for inspiration, and add to it each time.

Next job....find a room to rent. I started by looking in the local paper, asking friends if they knew of anything going. This did lead to a few viewings, but none were really suitable. At this point I will say sit down and think about what type of room you want and the location and how much you can afford: this will save a lot of time and energy. After quite a few letters to local businesses and finding great rooms but not at the right price (some people want at least 45% of what you take - I was stunned!), and getting despondent, I thought "Well, try the Law of Attraction: think about what you want and the universe will provide". To my amazement it did. It all happened when by chance I walked in to a local chiropractor to see if they had any rooms. I got talking to the receptionist about my business and what I needed; sure enough he put me in touch with a friend who wanted to let out one of her rooms. It was just what I wanted and we agreed on 25%, which she would reduce when I got busy. Yes, at last someone willing to help! I really am into believing this Law of Attraction.

Clients please

So I had the room, now I needed clients: what is the best way of getting clients?

Not having a lot of spare cash behind me, I decided to try and do a website on my own. Sure enough, there are many web-building sites out there, but after a few weeks of slogging I realised there was a lot more to this than I could manage, so I got my brother to create my website. Looking back, this was a mistake: get your website done professionally so that you can get it to the top of the ratings quickly for people to find you.

Next I tried posters and flyers; all very good, but they can be expensive and, being in the "holistic" category, I've found people like to hear about what I do; sometimes they've never heard of the treatment and if they have they want to know more about it. I found that getting out there and talking to people or word of mouth from existing clients is definitely the best advertising ever.

I then set about trying to find places where I could give a talk about what I do, and again the chiropractor came up trumps and suggested that I gave an evening about pain relief. This was so exciting - they even advertised it to their customers and got a group of people to turn up for me; how amazing is that? So all I had to do was attend and give the talk. I must admit it was nerve-racking, having never spoken in public before, but it turned out fine. I talked about what I do, so don't be afraid to challenge yourself, get out there and have fun doing it. There was no stopping me now: I got 2 clients from that evening and I couldn't wait to do another. After a few weeks a lady who had attended the evening rang to see if I would do a charity evening where we could do mini-sessions. All the money would be going to charity, but again it would cost me nothing but my time and hopefully there would be a lot of potential clients. This was a great evening; I got to talk to lots of people and sure enough over the weeks I obtained 4 clients, so definitely not a waste of time, and as they say "every little helps".

The talk

The next big thing to happen out of the blue was that I had a phone call from a local doctor who was a husband of one of my clients and she had recommended me to him, asking if I would like to do a talk for the doctors' training course he was running, I cannot tell you how excited I was; it was short notice because someone had dropped out so I only had two weeks to prepare for a four-hour talk. What an experience! I was so worried I would not fill the time, but hey, once you get me talking hours just fly by! It was a great success and I so enjoyed doing it. Please, please, if you get the opportunity to do this kind of thing go for it - you will have a great time. This then led to me getting referrals from this doctor's practice and from the doctors attending the course: "priceless".

I cannot express this strongly enough: talk to everybody and anybody about what you do. I have had so many clients this way. Even if they don't need you, I bet they know someone who does, and if they feel they can trust you, they will recommend you. I tell everyone I can - shop assistants, hairdressers, beauticians, everyone - get them to spread the word about you. I have a few hairdressing friends who have passed clients my way and I return the favour if I can; this all helps to promote you. Also phone or visit local organisation or schools to see if they would be interested in having you go along to give a demonstration and talk; these are always interesting.

Getting motivated when work is slow is always hard - you can always find ways to be distracted. So make a goal list for the day; I found this keeps me more focused and productive. Sitting at the computer and emailing old clients with new promotions or enquiring how they've been since you saw them last can get you new work, and having a newsletter to send out is a good way of keeping in touch with people.

So the adventure is still ongoing...the mountain can be tough sometimes, but I always try to rise to the challenge and have reached many of the goals I first set out to achieve. I can say the best of times far outweigh the worst.

May your adventure be as fulfilling as mine...

Julie Thompson Crawley: www.bedford-hypnosis-nlp. co.uk

• The Beginning – And a New Beginning

Well here you are. After years of studying you finally have those qualifications you have been working so hard to attain. You have achieved everything you set out to achieve.

All of that time learning a new skill and absorbing many hours of study and knowledge; you now stand on the threshold. This is it; the time to begin to practise and see people for real. No more classroom role plays or using friends as case studies: this is it, the real thing.

For others of you, "graduation" may seem a long time away. You're already in practice, you're seeing clients – but maybe not very many and sometimes it feels like you're attending to more "family and friends" than you bargained for.

So let's ask you: does it feel like you thought it would? After all, you have worked so hard in getting here, does it feel like "here" is where you want to be right now and does it feel like here is how you imagined here would feel?

For sure a mixture of emotions are running through you right now. A combination of excitement mixed with trepidation and some fear thrown in for good measure.

The good news is most newly-qualified practitioners – and even those who have been in practice for some time - feel exactly as you are right now. That confidence that once seemed very apparent has slipped quietly into the shadows, along with whole chunks of the knowledge you obtained through all those years of study.

Of course this isn't the case, and is only the mild anxiety that we all feel when we come out of our comfort zone and approach something new.

In your case your comfort zone being the safety of your university, training centre or college - now that's no longer there your nervousness and apprehension are no different from someone starting a new job for the first time. This is most definitely how you need to reframe those niggling fears, as they really are only playing with you.

You are embarking upon a new beginning; if you're reading this book it is safe to say the likelihood is you are either starting your own private CAM practice on the way to becoming a fully-fledged professional practitioner, or you are an existing practitioner and you know your practice isn't all you dreamt it would be.

Many of us have come into the complementary and alternative health professions because we've had our own personal challenges in the past and now feel it is right to help others as we were. This sense of cause and determination regularly drives practitioners to achieve the results they want in clinical practice and can also generate a great sense of purpose and achievement – when it all works and you get to add value to other people's lives.

As we find ourselves together at this point we are going to work on the basis that you have made up your mind and are looking to set up your own practice in a way that will be efficient, effective – and fun!

Yes fun! This is the fun part of going into business for yourself. We have many fond memories of wandering around town looking for rooms, designing stationery and creating our first websites. It was all so exciting! We're envious of you all, whether it's a beginning or a new beginning for you setting up your own successful practice.

• Different Ways of Setting Up

When setting up your first practice there are some very important considerations and some important decisions you have to make.

One of the first business decisions for you is how you intend to trade. There are a number of options and each has different advantages and disadvantages and levels of complexity. Let's look at them each in turn so you can clearly see the benefits and potential setbacks of each.

Sole Trader

The Pros:

- Being a sole trader is the simplest way to run a business - it does not involve paying any registration fees, keeping records and accounts is straightforward and you get to keep all the profits. However, you are personally liable for any debts that your business runs up. All you need to do is inform the Inland Revenue you are trading.

- You make all the decisions on how to manage your business.
- You raise money for the business out of your own assets and/or with loans from banks or other lenders.
- You must keep records showing your business income and expenses.
- Any profits go to you.
- Your profits are taxed as income.
- You need to register for Self Assessment and complete a tax return each year. As of today you can do this yourself and don't have to employ an accountant.

The Cons:

- A downside may be you are not taken as seriously as a limited company.
- As a sole trader, you are personally responsible for any debts run up by your business. This means your home or other assets may be at risk if your business runs into trouble.
- All self-employed practitioners take out liability insurance to safeguard against any eventualities. (The Holistic Insurance Company is a credible insurer offering value for money and can accommodate the needs of most practitioners.)

Limited Company

There are broadly two types of private company:

- private limited company
- private unlimited company

A private limited company may be limited by shares or by guarantee. A company is an unlimited company if there is no limit on the liability of its members.

The Pros:

- It is common to issue shares in a limited company to restrict the liability if anything was to go wrong. For example, the company could issue shares – let's say 100, valued at £10 each. The total liability of the company is therefore £1000.00.
- Your own personal liability is therefore limited to the money you have put in and the value of the company.
- Because you have set up a limited company you effectively work for the company as an employee, which vastly reduces any personal risk or potential loss. This is one of the advantages of setting up in this way.
- You are always taken seriously by clients and business partners.
- There are also potential tax advantages if you set up in this way compared to being a sole trader.

The Cons:

- There needs to be a formal structure in place and more administration and timescales to be adhered to. You can be fined if Inland Revenue deadlines aren't met.
- It is also advisable to have an accountant looking after your financial affairs, which is an extra cost.

Partnerships

There are three types of partnership:

- ordinary partnerships
- limited partnerships
- limited liability partnerships (LLPs)

All three types of partnership have the following features in common:

- Two or more persons – ie the partners - share the risks, costs and responsibilities of being in business.
- The profits and gains of the partnership are shared among the partners, unless the partnership agreement states otherwise.
- Each partner is personally responsible for paying tax on their share of the profits and gains, and for their National Insurance contributions.
- Each partner must register for Self Assessment with HM Revenue & Customs (HMRC) and complete an annual tax return.
- The partnership must keep records showing business income and expenses.

It's a good idea to draw up a written agreement between the partners. For further advice, consult an accountant or solicitor. If a partner leaves the partnership, the remaining partners may be liable for the entire debt of the partnership. Therefore, partners do not enjoy any protection if the business fails.

It is common for a new practitioner to set up as a sole trader to begin with. After trading for a while often it is common to change the set-up to that of a limited company.

It is important that anybody starting in business for the first time considers all the options and choose the option they feel most comfortable with and the one that meets the needs of themselves and their business.

*For more information: www.businesslink.gov.uk, www.companieshouse.gov.uk. Also see "Working for yourself: An Entrepreneur's guide to the basics", by Jonathan Reuvid (Kogan page, 2009).

• **Insurance & Liability**

When we discuss professional bodies later on you will understand how important it is to join the professional body that governs your type of therapy or discipline. A requirement of all professional bodies is that you have the appropriate insurance to be able to practise safely.

Insurance is something you must have. It is so important that trading without it isn't an option. In the Complementary and Alternative Medicine arena, depending on your trading discipline, it often isn't expensive and can start from around £50 a year. There are several types of insurance that you may need.

Professional indemnity

This type of insurance is very important and covers you against any claims you may face as a result of your work, or any treatments carried out. It covers you against damages and injury if a client or patient makes a claim against you. Under no circumstances should you begin practising without it.

The premiums vary depending on the nature of the work that you do. Most insurers offer a variety of choices of levels of cover and often will cover a variety of therapies on one single policy

Public Liability

Public liability covers exactly what is says on the tin. It covers you in case anyone visiting you at your place of work suffers an accident or injury while on your premises.

It is not mandatory or a legal requirement, however think of the potential problems that could arise if you don't have it.

Many practitioners work from home. If this is your situation, simply check with your household insurer if there is an option to include it on your household policy

Product Liability

Product liability applies if you are retailing, recommending or selling products as part of your practice.

This can potentially get complicated, especially if you are recommending or selling someone else's products.

A good example would be when a nutritional therapist recommends nutritional supplements to clients. If a client has a bad reaction they may look to progress legal action against the therapist. It is always difficult in these circumstances as liability has to be established. If the product was sealed when given and faulty in some way then generally the liability lies with the retailer.

It works in exactly the same way if herbs have been prescribed or recommended. If they are faulty in some way the manufacturer is generally held liable.

If there has been negligence in the recommendation then blame can be directed at the practitioner

Employer's Liability

This covers for any accident or claim made by employees while on your premises. It is a legal requirement and is automatically built into business insurance packages.

Motor Insurance

It is mandatory in the UK to have motor insurance if you have a motor vehicle, but as a business owner it is highly possible you will be using your vehicle in connection with your business. You will need to advise your motor insurer as they will need to add business use to your policy.

The cost of this normally is based upon the amount of business mileage you do and whether or not you are using your vehicle to transport clients or products.

Limited business use is generally given free of charge and is called class 1 business use. Class 2 and above however can cost an additional 25% and upwards, depending on the insurer.

Please make sure you advise your insurer as soon as you begin practising; you may need to shop around at this point to get the best deal for you.

Permanent health insurance

This type of insurance replaces long term income if you are unable to work. It is very expensive and often has exclusions built in for the self- employed, depending on profession.

Its sole purpose is to replace income, often until retirement, so ensure you are clear about exclusion clauses on the policy. These often take the form of deferred periods that can be as long as 12 months, so get properly informed before you insure against long term health problems. Insurance premiums for this are normally paid monthly and there is a limit on how much cover you can have depending on your income.

Of course, as CAM practitioners we trust that we know a thing or two about keeping healthy. Health insurance is in effect a bet that you can only win by losing. You "win" – you get something for all those premiums you've paid – by losing your health. If you are a true believer then you will make the case that your money is better spent on good quality food, nutritional and herbal supplements, and regular CAM treatments to help keep yourself in peak shape. On the other hand, accidents happen, and while the NHS will scrape you up and treat you, without insurance you will lose your income, and that could be catastrophic.

Personal accident insurance

Personal accident insurance pays out a lump sum of money if you claim as a result of an accident. The premiums for these policies are paid annually and often carry much exclusion.

Business insurance packages

When you are operating your business from your own centre it is common to take out a business insurance policy which can include buildings and contents insurances and a range of liability insurances such as those detailed above.

Legal insurance

Legal fees can be very expensive, so it is advisable to have legal advice and expenses cover. In an increasingly litigious society (thanks America for teaching us this one), there is some truth in the idea that you are more likely to be sued than have an accident or end up in hospital. Businesses are especially vulnerable. This type of insurance can often be included in various business memberships – eg the Federation of Small Businesses.

• Professional Bodies

When you set up your own private practice it is extremely important that you join the appropriate professional body.

Your discipline-specific professional organisation will often be able to provide you details of all that you need to run a successful practice, including insurance, and will also allow you to display their professional logo on your own website, adding professionalism and credibility to your business.

It is common for your university or course provider to be accredited by different professional bodies. It is advisable to start here and investigate thoroughly whom they recommend you join.

It is important to recognise from the outset there are many professional bodies for each therapeutic discipline and you should join the ones that meet several criteria. These include regular communication (at least monthly), with some kind of method for keeping you updated with ongoing changes and learning and practice requirements, including continuing professional development (CPD) opportunities.

It is also sensible to join the professional body that has a good membership package and is a leading voice in your specific therapeutic discipline. On top of that, join one of the "umbrella" organisations that represent different types of CAM practitioners – there is strength in numbers.

The world of CAM is always changing and it is vital you keep up to speed with how these changes affect your individual practice. These days, the leading professional bodies are often engaged on many different levels. These include sitting on government and industry steering groups helping your own discipline to progress and change in line with regulatory changes. And it is becoming common to join a number of professional bodies especially if you are practising more than one therapeutic discipline.

In addition the largest industry leading professional bodies are perceived as centres of excellence and are the first place potential clients look for when searching for a practitioner. These organisations by now should all have a list of registered members available online so that potential clients can find the practitioner of their choice. The more advanced enable individual practitioners to have their own profile space to display all their professional details and qualifications.

• Premises

When deciding on where you are going to set up you need to give a lot of thought to a number of key factors. If you just jump on the first idea that comes to you, you may end up regretting it farther down the line. Here are the questions you need to answer:

- Does your business rely upon passing trade?
- What is your target market for clients?
- How are you going to gain the credibility you need to attract your target market?
- Where is the best location to attract the most clients?
- Do you want a multi-centre practice?
- Do you want to work from home?
- Are you OK working on your own, or would you prefer to have other practitioners around you?
- Where is your nearest competition?
- How are clients going to get to your practice?
- Is there sufficient parking?
- Logistically is it easy to find and reach you?
- Should you base your clinic in a location known for your type of work, e.g. Harley Street?
- What is your budget for renting premises?

Renting a Room

By far the easiest and cheapest option. When negotiating on terms of the let, make sure you are only responsible for rent when you use the room. Some landlords like a monthly fixed rent whether you are there or not. Others are happy to agree a percentage of your fee when you actually use the room. They then invoice you for the time you have used.

It's common to expect to negotiate between 10% and 25% of your fee. There are odd exceptions in certain locations - Harley Street, for example - where they generally charge a fixed fee per hour.

The room and location must match the profile and branding of your business, as credibility and reputation are paramount to your future success. Don't "make do". For example, if you are a physiotherapist, chiropractor, nutritional therapist or counsellor, having a connection with or a room at a private clinic or doctor's surgery would give you credibility and give you that professional edge over your competition.

It is also important that the room is quiet, easy to get to and that there is plenty of parking for clients. In addition it needs to have a reception area (you don't need a receptionist) and facilities such as refreshments, water and toilets should all be easily available.

Avoid signing long leases and when asked to sign a room agreement; study the paperwork with care

Working from home

Yes, this is a valid option. Many practitioners have worked from home at some point. Once again you have to look at the overall "proposition" of your business – the sense of style and quality you want to project, for instance - and decide whether seeing clients or patients at home fits with the profile of your business, or with your industry.

It is important to put yourselves in the shoes of the client and ask yourself how you would feel going to someone's house to receive a treatment. How professional do you think it is and will it meet your client's expectations of the service they are coming for? If you are seriously considering this option, get an objective second opinion from someone you trust to be honest and have them do a "walk through". Get them to park in your street, walk up your pathway, enter your house and walk to the room you are going to use. What's their impression? There will undoubtedly be clutter that has to be moved, maybe some redecoration and safety-angled repairs needed as well. Remember, you must make a good impression and you do want your clients to feel comfortable and well-looked after.

Working from home presents other challenges and can affect your own levels of motivation and commitment. You can start to feel very isolated working at home; going into a rented room in a town puts you in touch with other people and gives a change of scenery.

Leasing a clinic or practice room

This is another popular option, but normally more appropriate when the practice has been established for a while and has sufficient (healthy) turnover to make this possible financially. If you have one or two other practitioners you are going into practice with and can agree on who gets which days, then that also makes this a runner.

The problem is that leasing a set of rooms for a clinic/ practice incurs a number of charges and you need to be confident your business is profitable enough to meet the demands of the lease for the whole period of the lease. The duration of commercial property lets tends to vary from 12 months to 6 years. The longer the lease, the more negotiating power you normally have.

It is normally advisable to insist on a tenant-only break-out clause halfway through the term, and also protection over unreasonable rate increases at the end of the term. This is done by building into the original lease an indexed only rate increase. This means the rent can only go up in line with inflation or the retail price index. This is known as indexation.

Let's examine the costs involved:

- Annual rent for term of lease - as a guide 100 square feet = £1,000 a year
- Business rates - based upon the size of your premises. N/A currently on ratable values under £6,000 a year
- Buildings and contents insurance- charged pro rata with other tenants
- Public liability insurance
- All utility bills such as gas and electricity
- Maintenance fees for any communal areas
- Car parking costs
- Business phone, broadband and IT costs
- Legal fees in setting up the lease

Example: The rental of a room 15ft by 15ft.

Total square footage = 225 sq ft:
225 x 1000 = £2250 PA =   £187.50 per month
Electricity   £ 60.00 per month
Water   £ 30.00 per month
Phone   £ 50.00 per month
Broadband   £ 25.00 per month
Rates N/A under £6000
Buildings insurance   £ 20.00 per month
Contents insurance   £ 15.00 per month
Public liability   £ 5.00 per month
Parking   £ 35.00 per month
Maintenance communal charge   £ 30.00 per month
Legal fees   £ 25.00 per month

Total £482.50 x 12 =   £5790 per annum

Joint Ventures

It often seems like a good idea to go into business with somebody else - perhaps another practitioner with a different therapeutic discipline.

You can split costs and get referrals from each other. Just be sure if you do this the commercial branding of both businesses complement each other, as if they don't you can put off potential clients. We will look at this in more depth later on

• Setting up your Clinic

When setting up it is important to write a business plan and have business goals. You know from what Julie Thompson Crawley had to say that this can be really inspiring! We will look at that in more detail in the next section; for now, we're going to look at how you can set up your clinic space and your practice administration procedures, with particular focus on dealing with clients and record-keeping. On one level you need to do this formally to ensure you adhere to any appropriate data protection and confidentiality laws; on another level you will find that if you get this right – and we will tell you how – it will save you stacks of time and help you keep on top of your clients' needs.

Practice essentials

You need to start thinking about how you want your practice to look and feel to your clients. It is important that you ensure the "client experience" is the best it can be. We've probably all had the rather unnerving experience of going to see a highly recommended practitioner or specialist who operates out of grubby, run-down premises.

There are some genius practitioners who can get away with it, but for most of us we need to make sure that every impression the client gets – from the outside of the building, through the reception area and into and including, especially, the layout and decorative order of your room communicates the professionalism of your practice and enhances your profile.

Think seriously about office furniture such as a desk and comfortable chairs, sofa and client facilities such as exactly the right sort of examination table or bodywork couch: these are all fundamental and important in creating the right look and feel of your practice.

Plants, candles, pictures, soft music, all add to creating the right ambience for your practice. Ensure there are toilet facilities and that phones have a divert facility and/or can be silenced. It is also important to consider road noise or any other possible interruptions that may interfere with your ultimate goal of creating the right client experience.

In addition it is important to be able to offer the client water, tea, coffee or herbal tea. Having a jug of fresh water on the table with attractive glasses is a must in any professional practice.

You will see the term "client experience" a lot throughout this book. It's our shorthand for a way of reminding you to always be thinking about things from the perspective of your ideal client: the type of client who not only becomes a regular, but champions you and your practice to everyone they know. You need to keep that ideal client in mind at all times in the embryonic stages of setting up your practice and beyond.

Client stationery - the client process

It is important to establish a robust system for managing appointments, records and notes and any follow-up booking of appointments or invoicing that needs to happen.

Let's look at this in a logical order of the client process as it normally happens; then it is easy to see what you will need in place to make sure the client moves through the sequence methodically and finds it all easy to comply with.

1. Client books an appointment
2. Client needs directions and travel tips to your practice
3. You require basic client information before the appointment
4. Client arrives for their appointment
5. You need formal client consent to work together
6. You need to confirm basic client info and if necessary take a formal case history
7. Appointment conducted and records of appointment documented
8. Client makes a follow-up appointment
9. Client needs facility to pay for their session

It is vitally important you have this process in place before you start seeing clients and although some view this as complicated, if you have a set process from day 1 it makes it a lot easier from then on and becomes habitual for you as the practitioner.

So let's look at the above and work through what you need.

1. **Client books an appointment**
   You need a diary system in place to log the appointment and a way to collect name, address and contact info.

2. **Client needs directions to find your practice**
   You need directions on your website or the facility to email directions and travel tips, parking instructions and so on direct to the client.

3. **You may require info from client before the appointment**
   You need to send client a questionnaire for completion before they see you.

4. **Client arrives for their appointment**
   You need the facility to offer refreshments and any client comforts that are necessary.

5. **You need formal client consent to work together**
   Ask client to sign a client consent form - some practitioners include this on their client record card, completed once at the first appointment with any client.

6. **You need to confirm basic client info**
   You need to be able to complete a client record card registering all personal and logistical details of client.

7. **Appointment conducted and records of appointment documented**
   You need a note-taking facility such as a session notes form to complete with the client during the session that may be signed by the client at the end.

8. **Client makes a follow-up appointment**
   Get this appointment in the diary before your client leaves their first appointment. There is a large fall-out of second appointments if this doesn't happen. We will look at this in detail later on.

9. Client needs facility to pay for their session

You need to be able to take and receipt cash, cheque or credit card, or send an invoice for payment post-session.

It is easy to see following these nine clear steps what stationery you will need to conduct a client interview. We are going to look at the client process in more detail later on, but for now just get a grasp of the basic forms you will need before seeing clients:

- Diary and Appointment system
- Health Questionnaire
- Client goal sheet
- Client Consent Form
- Client Record Card
- Session Notes Form
- Invoice and Receipt

Other Stationery

- Practice letter-headed paper
- Business Cards
- Business Leaflets
- Client Foolscap Files
- Photocopy paper
- Envelopes
- Accounts Ledger
- Posters
- Paper

Office Hardware

Office hardware will differ from practice to practice, budget to budget. However there are certain things every practitioner needs to run a commercially successful practice. These include

- Filing cabinet(s)
- Computer
- Decent printer
- Landline telephone
- Mobile phone that includes email and diary
- Table and Chairs
- Desk
- Shredder
- Couch

Office Software

This would include:

- A Customer Management System
- A website
- A practice email address
- A designated business and mobile telephone number
- A PO Box number or business address
- Skype conferencing facility
- Microsoft Outlook diary software
- Microsoft Office

Practice Management Software

All successful practitioners have a robust system to manage all facets of their businesses, from appointment-making to invoicing to record-keeping. This is often done manually to keep costs down.

Very recently a new software package was launched specifically for therapists and practitioners (PPM Software Ltd, 01992 655940, www.ppmsoftware.com).

For a small set-up fee and around £100 per month (at time of writing) you can invest in a system that will take care of all of your office administration and client management. This includes all record keeping, backing up of client files, invoicing, account reconciliation and much more.

Another system, eHealth, has been designed specifically for nutritional therapists (NTs), although it could be used by other CAM practitioners. Developed by, among others, one of the UK's leading practitioners Ben Brown, ND, it walks you through everything you need to do with a client, even starting by generating a Letter of Engagement for the client to sign – a requirement of the NT's professional body which sets out exactly what the therapist can and cannot do. It aims to streamline patient management, business, marketing, and accountancy so that the CAM practitioner can focus on the clinical end of things. (eHealth Practice Management Software: http://ehealthpractice. co.uk)

Client communication

Practitioners can sometimes be very subjective when it comes to ways of communicating with clients and often base their views on their own preferences or experiences.

But client communication is key to the successful running of any practice and it's important to be able to reach and communicate with our clients in the way that suits them the most. These days that can include email, social media such as LinkedIn, Twitter and Facebook, telephone sessions on Skype (www.skype.com), face to face, webinar, podcast, even via text messaging.

Equally important, you need to be able to see your client when they want to be seen. This often involves weekends and evenings. Most people work all day so an evening or weekend is the only option.

Data Protection - The Data Protection Act 1988

If you handle personal information about individuals, you have a number of legal obligations to protect information and ensure all your client records are confidential. You have to be able to prove you have taken the appropriate steps.

As practitioners it's not enough for you to make sure that everything your client shares with you stays with you, but you must also make sure that any records of your consultations, or any other information you hold about the client is also confidential.

This involves some simple steps like always keeping client records locked away in secure filing cabinets and securing and password protecting any back-up files held on your computer. Many practitioners also use a simple code to label client files and keep names and addresses separately, so names cannot be matched to notes if files are lost, stolen or mislaid.

When keeping client records and information it is a legal requirement you abide by the Data Protection Act of 1988. The Act confirms if you are holding data then you need to register with the Information Commissioner's Office (ICO). This is the UK's independent authority set up to uphold information rights in the public interest, promoting openness by public bodies and data privacy for individuals. Everyone in business holding client data and records needs to register with the ICO and pay an annual membership fee. This is around £40 a year. There are a small number of exemptions for charities, pension funds and voluntary organisations.

* www.ico.gov.uk

Keeping Client Records

There are conflicting reports of how long we need to keep client records. The textbook answer is you need to keep them for a year longer than a client would be able to sue you for negligent advice (or for breach of contract); so that works out to 7 years from the final letter to the client or final action on the client file.

You are legally obliged to hold client records for a minimum of six years in addition to the 12 months potential for legal action.

Chapter 2: Researching your practice

That wasn't so bad, was it?

We've covered the basics of setting up your practice like a successful business.

If you follow that step-by-step programme, you can relax. A bit. You know you have the basic systems in place so that you are legally OK to start seeing clients and can collect their information and get paid.

In this chapter we're going to go a little deeper into positioning your practice to attract the business you want and deserve, and also explain how you can learn from other people's successes (and failures) in a way that will make an immediate, direct impact on how you do things.

As a trained CAM practitioner you know all about research. That's what informed your training. You went at it to write your projects and/or dissertation. And you probably did a fair amount before you even decided where to start your education. Well, get ready to get stuck in again – this time with research into your own practice – where it should be, what services you should offer, and what is the best way to present your message.

• Research Model – SLEPT

Before starting any new business or stepping out into a new phase of your existing business, you must do your "due diligence" - research and analysis. When conducting this research you need to have a clear vision of what your practice is going to look like and the type of clients you are hoping to attract.

All your research should focus on the Big 5:

1. The Client
2. The Service
3. The Practitioner
4. Market size
5. The Competition

And everything you do in relation to the Big 5 has to be what Mark always refers to as "the difference that makes the difference". Your proposition has to be better than all of the competition around you. You must aim to offer a service to your client that is second to none. We'll come back to this later on.

Visiting potential practice rooms, finding the right location, researching competitors and formulating your personal business vision and model all adds up not only to an enlightening experience but is great fun as well. But the serious side is that you have to get this right if you are going to form the foundations of a successful future business.

With the power of the Internet there is very little we can't find out quite quickly, so what you might initially think would take weeks to research in reality can just take a day or two.

When conducting research The **SLEPT** model is as good as any to use as a framework for business analysis.

SLEPT simply breaks down the different and important areas of research to:

Social
Legislative
Economic
Political
Technology

Often most of us wouldn't have the business skills or knowledge to even think about these key five areas of potential impact let alone research and plan around them. **SLEPT** enables us to research confidently outside the world of the clinic and look objectively at high impact influences that will influence the success or failure of our business going forward. Let's look at this in more depth.

Social

This enables us to look at how our market is growing and establish any trends that may help or assist with our business development. For example, we know that between 2007 and 2009 the Complementary Medicine market increased by 18% and is still on the up, a lot of it down to public awareness and regulatory change. Therefore this indicates this is a good time to enter this market.

Legislation

Rules and regulations are always changing and evolving as the world of complementary medicine and talking therapies moves further and further towards potentially full regulation in the future.

On top of that, many CAM practitioners need to know the impact of new EU legislation on the availability of nutritional supplements and herbal remedies.

Ensure you understand the implications of current legislation and the future impact it may have on your business. Ensure your training and qualifications meet the requirements of the day and keep abreast of change. Your professional body should be on top of this.

Two other great resources for the latest info are CAM magazine, where Simon makes sure practitioners are kept informed by news stories and features and interviews with those directly involved in legislation (www.cam-mag.com) and the Alliance for Natural Health (http://anh-europe.org).

Economic

Understand the current and ongoing economic situation and how this may impact on your business. This doesn't mean you have to subscribe to "The Economist" and start reading the "heavy" newspapers, but simply means spending some time looking for health-related economic stories and statistics.

For example, there has been a rise in work-related stress conditions and mental health disorders are on the increase; the economic impact on businesses and the NHS is often being reported. What this means is that there demands and opportunities for practitioners who can address this issue is increasing.

Political

This relates to changes in government influence which can directly influence and effect new businesses and new initiatives. For example, the UK government is launching a new initiative to support and encourage entrepreneurs and new business start-ups. There are often many other initiatives happening at local government and regional level. Get tuned into these.

Technology

As technology progresses and develops we can reach more people ore quickly and can establish a national presence within months.

With the right knowledge and marketing skills you can reach your target audience via Google, social media, and data-based marketing campaigns in the first few months of setting up. You don't need to be a geek to take advantage, but you do need to be up to speed with what's possible.

• The Importance of a Website

Almost everybody checks out practitioners on the web. Even if someone they know has recommended you. Some clients have told us they won't even do business with anyone who doesn't have a web presence. So we're including websites right up front as part of the fundamental setting-up stage. Your website needs to be in place and ready to go as you begin to practise.

A lot of practitioners don't have a website at the set-up stage of their businesses. The reasons – or should we say misconceptions – they have for this include:

- It's too expensive
- I don't need one
- It's too complicated
- The time's not right. I know someone who'll do it when I'm ready. (Procrastination)
- They don't understand websites - we are afraid of what we don't understand.
- Leaflets and posters will be just as good to get my name out there.

Let's look at some of the facts about websites:

- 88% of people buy online – and this number is increasing all the time
- Websites provide information and a service immediately in response to a client request. We are in the request and response business and speed is of the essence
- We live in a world where the largest communication tool is the Internet
- The average start-up price for a professional website is as little as £50 with £10.00 per month as an ongoing management fee (Figures from Web heeler ltd, who provide bespoke and specialised websites

for the alternative medicine practitioner community - 0870 757 9878, www.webheeler.net)
- With a website you can communicate information about your services to anywhere in the world
- You can change your website whenever you want to, to reflect changes in your business
- You can run website advertising campaigns to put you at the top of Google at minimal costs, therefore exposing your new business immediately to a wide audience
- It takes three to six months for your website to organically reach competitive ratings on Google, so it important to set one up as a priority - even before you begin practicing

---

Mark's Modelling Tip

We'll explain about modelling soon enough, but for now what we want to get across is that whenever we flag up a modelling tip from Mark, this refers to something that Mark has personally used and tested with business clients he has coached.

He has coached thousands of businesses over the years and developed a simple strategy for success. All his advice and recommendations – which we are sharing in this book – have been proven in practice to work.

Ensuring you have a live website from day 1 falls into this category.

How should your website look?

First, be clear about how you see and feel about how your business will look and feel. As importantly, think about how you want your business to be perceived by your future audience.

Once you have established this, use Google to investigate other practitioners operating in similar markets to you. You will find a number of websites you like the look and feel of. Notice how many pages and different sections these websites have, which colours are used, and in particular the layout and visual effects.

Once you have done this, choose a website provider that meets your budget and can provide structural templates, hosting, and Search Engine Optimization services.

This is a very simple way to start your practice with your first website and will ensure you get cost effective service and control over the timescales to set the website up. Using a professional template means you simply have to decide on what pages you will have and how you will structure each page. A year or two down the line as your business evolves and you have a larger dedicated budget you may wish to try new and more advanced website techniques

Important note – free and nearly-free websites

There are many providers of free websites that seem to offer very attractive propositions. From our own experience we can say you only ever get what you pay for; keep this in mind when making your decision.

That said, when you absolutely, positively HAVE to get a website up right now with the minimum fuss and cost, look at services like Vistaprint, the business card people. We've used them in the past. With a charge for the basic package of only just over £3, you can have a site up almost instantaneously – and its template can even match your business cards. It's a good stop-gap measure. (www.vistaprint.co.uk)

By the way, to reinforce our message about websites, Vistaprint's slogan runs: "85% of people contact businesses they find in local searches. That's why 100% of businesses need a website."

Websites - where do I start?

Here's what you are looking for:

1 **Reliable Hosting Service** - someone to rent you the space on their server, ie a place to put your site

2 **Search Engine Optimisation Services** - a process to help get you to the top of Google's rankings ASAP

3 **A professional template** - a ready-made designed website and individual pages ready for you to type in your personal information

4 **The ability to make changes to your site yourself** - a must-have, as getting someone else to do this in time with your new ideas and desired changes is very difficult and can also be expensive

5 **Domain and email purchase and renewal** – a place to register the name of your website and associated email address; these are often included in hosting packages

You can find hosting services easily enough using Google. Search using the terms "best" and/or "reviews". You will find sites such as http://www.top10bestwebsitehosting. com which ranks hosting services according to a number of criteria.

If this is your first website and your knowledge is limited, you may find it easiest to approach a provider that specialises in your chosen field and offers bespoke website packages and services that meet all of your needs. Explain your requirements (as explained in 1 - 5 above) and they will guide you to the most appropriate package for you which will meet all your needs

A package such as this will incur the following typical costs

A template set-up cost	£ 50.00PA
Hosting charges	£ 60.00PA
Search Engine Optimisation	£ 60.00PA
Domain name and email	£ 10.00PA

Total Cost   **£180PA**

These websites provide a cost-effective, simple to operate, and speedy set up time, often you are up and running within a few days and your site is climbing Google's ladder within just a few months.

Pros and Cons of purpose-built templates

Pros:

- The provider will often offer bespoke services in line with your practitioner discipline
- You can select the template of choice from a library of several hundred templates
- The ability to provide a package ideal for first-time website owners
- Cost-effective with limited set-up costs and the ability to pay monthly
- The ability to make changes to your website whenever you choose
- All of your requirements within one easy to manage package and cost
- Ideal for inexperienced practitioners with limited technical knowledge

Cons:

- As your business grows you may demand more of your website. These packages can handle most of

today's demands, however complicated audio and visual requirements can reach a point beyond the capability of some website package providers.
- Inability to get the exact design you want due to Limited templates

Creating your own website with a Website Designer

Another option is to find a designer you like and ask them to design your website for you. This could take some time, as often designers have many projects on the go at the same time. (One we've used is www.soulbat.co.uk, 01435 5813082.)

Pros and Cons of designing your own website

Pros:

- You are in control over the entire design of your website
- You can tell your designer exactly what you want and have it
- You have the opportunity to create your business branding and profile with logos etc completely in line with your business philosophy, vision and mission

Cons:

- This option is more expensive and can cost between £500 - £5000
- You may have to pay SEO and hosting costs separately
- The designer will often be the only person who can change your website and you will have to pay for his time for changes made
- You have no control over the time to design the site. This can sometimes take several months.

If you are in any doubt, explore both options; you can always cost both and see which one works for you. Good website designers will happily give you a proposal outlining all costs and benefits.

So once have decided on a website style and design,you need to think about what pages you are going to have. At this stage and keeping costs in mind you will only need a handful of pages. Here is an example of pages for your first website:

Page	Content
Home	Most Important Page. Details to include a summary of you, your services, your location, and any relevant PR such as points you want your clients to know and any testimonials. 95% of your SEO is taken from this page and many people checking out websites never get past the first page.

Simple SEO guidelines - Mention your location, services, and areas of expertise at least twice on the home page. |
| **About You** | All details about you, your qualifications, past experience, any details you feel are relevant and you want your potential client to know. Another good place for any appropriate PR about you, anything that may potentially sell you to future clients. Remember, people buy people; they always have and always will...they are less interested |

than you might think in your impressive qualifications – they are looking for a connection to you as a person. So be yourself, show a bit of personality, and do use an up to date and flattering picture of yourself.

Services Offered   A full list of what you have to offer.

Price and Policy   I believe it professional to be transparent with your potential clients about what you charge. So yes, publish your fees on your site. In addition you may wish to publish any other policy that is relevant - eg cancellation charges and so on

Contact   All contact details and hours of working. A good tip is to use Google maps and have this displayed at the bottom of your contact page so people know where to find you

Mark's Modelling Tip

Have your contact phone number and a direct click to your email at the top of every page in bold type and clearly visible to the site visitor.

Practitioner Case Study

Putting your website to work – and social media

In my line of work as a Nutritional Therapist, setting up a website was the first task on my "to-do" list. It is effectively your shop window to your marketplace that gives you the chance to explain what you do to your target audience in a very cost-effective way.

When I first embarked on designing my website I had to think carefully about how I wanted my customers to feel when they visited the site. What sort of image, brand and identity did I want to portray?

As a Nutritional Therapist I felt it was important to have a clean and crisp image using colours that evoked freshness and quenched the thirst of my clients. I went for an apple green colour with grey tones. The layout had to be user-friendly pages that clearly explained the different areas of my business. They were as follows: Home page, What is NT?, Benefits of NT, Who I am, Price & Policy, Make an Enquiry, Contact us.

The most important page, we all know, is the home page, as this is the first place your potential client lands. If the structure of your website is messy and not laid out clearly this just annoys the viewer and they will click off as quickly as they clicked on.

My homepage included where my clinic was, a brief write-up about me, the benefits of NT, what a client would receive in a consultation plus a box with the latest Health News. I also used eye-catching photos which I bought off the Internet. I laid this out into a format of two columns at the top of the page and three at the bottom, this way it looked clear, there was not too much writing and my viewer could read exactly what my business could offer them.

Promotions

Another idea I had was to include a Promotions box, which I could change regularly depending on what special offers I was offering at the time.

In order to attract the right clients to your business you need to give them something for free. In my line of work, offering a free health tip, a recipe of the month or latest news about product discounts can entice potential clients to sign up with their email address so that you can build a database. You can then send your whole list a newsletter with these freebies in each month and stay connected to them, without having to blindly hope they will return to your website.

The hardest part about a website is trying to reach the first page on the search engines. This is an area that you can tackle on your own using Google AdWords, if you know how, but equally there are a whole range of companies that offer this service too – for a fee.

Social media marketing is also easy to set up with Facebook, Twitter and LinkedIn, which lets everyone know what you are up to. This enables you to define your branding and identity in the marketplace, even if it's among your peer group and friends. Peer groups and friends also have friends and colleagues who have friends and colleagues and so on.

Social media marketing costs nothing and acts as a great word of mouth. If you wish to advertise with Facebook you can set up a business account to do this and direct your message to exactly who you want to. Facebook is brilliant at this and the payment options are extremely flexible. For instance, you could buy a small box advert which will feature at the side of Facebook accounts for as little as £20 for one week. As the potential customers click on it, it can take them to your website or Facebook page. Every click will cost you a fraction of the £20 that you have assigned to it. Clicks are more expensive if you select a wider audience, as it works as a supply and demand situation; if you reduce your target audience you can gain more clicks. In my case, having a small local clinic in Hitchin town centre, I only need to target the immediate area and a surrounding 10-mile radius.

Once you have your website set up you need to let people know your website address. I have printed this on all my business stationery and also applied to Google Maps with my details so that anyone searching for a Nutritional Therapist in Hertfordshire will see my clinic come up.

Karen Webb, Nutritional Therapist: www.lifepractice nutrition.co.uk

---

• Introduction to Modelling & NLP

Modelling is an exciting term from the world of NLP – Neuro-Linguistic Programming - with an even more exciting meaning and purpose. NLP is the study of excellence. The study of how a person excels in a particular skill or set of skills.

What does this mean?

Everyone has a skill that they excel at; something they are good at. NLP is a tool for accelerated learning. A person who has learnt NLP can choose to model someone with a skill or set of skills and achieve similar results - as if they had spent years practising the same skill. You can immediately see how this will relate to and benefit you and your practice.

What is the difference between NLP and other techniques for learning behaviors and skills?

Since the '70s NLP has evolved a set of tools that are specifically designed for learning about a person's behaviour through the unconscious uptake of their overt behaviors. The difference lies in identifying and understanding what the person is doing unconsciously and then building a reliable model of that person's behaviour. NLP provides the practitioner with tools to understand and map out a person's unconscious strategies and behaviours into a format that can be easily taught and learnt by anyone.

For example, someone might be in conversation with someone about money and happen to say, "Oh I never worry about money; I always have enough". An NLP practitioner, hearing that comment, would be absolutely fascinated. The question that would burst out of them would be, "How do you DO that?" This might lead into a detailed exploration of the person's thought processes, self-talk, beliefs, values and so on – or maybe simply identifying a unique way they spend and save - enabling the questioner, eventually, to "model" the way that person achieves financial happiness.

Is this all that NLP is, a tool for accelerated learning?

Though NLP started from modelling the therapeutic skills from three of its original proponents – the highly successful "miracle" psychotherapists Milton Erickson, MD, Virginia Satir and Fritz Perls - NLP has left in its wake a trail of tools and techniques that can be applied across the board to any form of human interaction.

This means a person who has learnt NLP can apply these skills into all areas of their life and achieve the results they desire. Commonly today you see NLP being applied to sport, the arts, politics, therapy, sales, leadership, dieting and really anything you can think of.

Where did it come from?

NLP was originally created by Dr John Grinder and Dr Richard Bandler in California in the 1970s. John at the time was an assistant professor of linguistics at UCLA and Richard a mathematician.

What does NLP consist of?

NLP consists of many models and techniques that can be applied to all areas of life, from how they relate to their loved ones and work colleagues to implementing the skills, techniques and attitudes for their own personal development and improvement.

Can anyone learn NLP?

Yes. NLP is not about theory, but about practicality; if you can talk about it, it doesn't mean you can do it. NLP is about having the skills and behaviors at the level of habit; that is your skills become a natural part of who you are.

Does this mean I will be more effective in my life?

Effective is a comparative word and difficult to define without a context or scenario. The way to be more effective is to have a wide range of skills that will enable you a greater chance of achieving whatever is your outcome. It is about being flexible with your behaviours and noticing if you are achieving your outcome or not. And if not to have the choice to choose another behaviour.

Is choice important in NLP?

Absolutely. Choice is not only important in NLP but in life. If you only have one way of doing something then you are stuck, if you have two ways then you are in a dilemma, with three ways you have choice. NLP provides the tools and means with which to increase your range of behaviours, thoughts and skills to have choice. To bring you closer to achieving those things you desire.

Think about your clinic and your clients just for a moment and write down all of the areas you think NLP might be able to help you run a successful practice.

Your list should include the following

- Building better client relationships
- Improving your interpersonal skills
- Enabling you to learn the art of perfect rapport
- Helping you control your client meetings
- Helping you motivate and inspire your clients
- Teaching you and your clients how to control your thinking patterns and subsequent behaviour
- Helping you align and identify with your clients' needs
- Increasing your confidence

Modelling - A detailed look

NLP Modelling is accelerated learning. NLP Modelling is the ability to fully replicate a desirable skill or behaviour that another person has by breaking it down into two discrete parts:

1) The full unconscious set of behaviours that perform the skill
2) The recognition and understanding of such behaviours in a teachable / learnable format

Modelling is at the heart of NLP; without it NLP would not exist.

Mark's Modelling Tip
Non-negotiable 1

Before embarking on any new business venture I would always embrace the key principles of modelling to guarantee my success as much as possible. I would have faith in the knowledge I was working a proven business model.

Focus on Successful Outcomes

Modelling is not concerned with "truth" or "theory"; to focus there would relegate the results to an impractical set of concepts better suited to discourse at the local winery. Modelling is concerned with the pragmatic outcome of achievable behavior: that is, the ability to replicate in full the behaviour of the person being modelled and be able to come up with teachable procedures so that others may learn them.

What does this mean?

If you know a person who performs extremely well in a particular setting and you would like to be able to have the same degree of grace and agility, presence and panache, then NLP Modelling is perhaps the most elegant method for acquiring that skill.

Natural Modellers

Children are natural modellers; they exhibit the quality of grandiose and exuberant curiosity without thought of the consequences or expectations of learning. They have a talent to learn at phenomenal rates, given the appropriate supportive conditions.

Given this, a child has the potential to learn anything. It has been shown that to learn a language, for instance, the early developmental environment must include people. People serve as a model from which to learn. Given that a child has no way of knowing how to construct a verbal language, without people to listen to and watch, to model, they would be unable to develop their language skills. A person passing through the school system is exposed to a system of learning information by instruction. To a child, this presents a different methodology of learning, one which demands they acquire new strategies in order to learn.

Some children do this successfully and others not so successfully. Yet the important point here is not that the child cannot learn, rather that the strategies they use to understand the information are acquired through trial and error and experience, through what they have been taught by their parents/guardians.

These new methods of learning will either help or hinder a child's progression through school and into adulthood as they attempt to learn through the methods employed by the schooling systems. When adulthood arrives the person has been entrained into using learning methods which may not have been appropriate for their own particular learning style, hence the reason why some people say "I'm not a good learner", "I was no good at school", or "I don't remember anything I was taught".

NLP Modelling is a method that re-teaches the person how to learn effectively, in the way that they were learning – or rather, just naturally and effortlessly soaking up new information - in their earlier stages of development.

Where can it be used?

NLP Modelling can be used in many different areas. Say you enjoy tennis and wish to improve your backhand. You know someone whose game is much better than yours and have noticed that they return the ball with their backhand exceptionally well.

By using NLP Modelling, you can learn how they do what they do and be able to have the same performance as that person, minus the differences in your own physiological makeup.

NLP Modelling is extremely useful for learning an ability that may have taken another person years to develop; you can learn it to the same level of performance that they exhibit. Think and relate this to the setting up of your practice.

How does it do this?

As we talked about earlier, NLP Modelling uses the same process of learning that you used as a child. The learning of a set of skills and techniques without any rationalisation or conscious intervention. This allows you, the modeller, to develop the necessary skills, behaviours, motor skills and unconscious processes that the other person has without trying to interpret what they do.

Children do not learn by rationalisation...if they did, they would probably stop before they began, because the rational approach would be.. "How can I move these thousands of muscles in sequence just to stand up?!" Similarly if you were to rationalise and unravel the process of learning complex and unconscious processes and strategies that the person has spent years developing, you would spend 10 times longer attempting to understand it.

So the essence of NLP Modelling is to NOT try to understand what you are wishing to learn at the level of consciousness, but to engage your unconscious resources by mirroring and matching the other person...or shadowing what they do.

How does this work?

We learn by observing patterns and differences.

Something that is repeated over and over again is said to have a "pattern". It is this pattern that tells us it is important, and the rest superfluous to our endeavors because there is only randomness to the information and therefore non-sense. For example, if you were to watch people who have outstanding relationships while they are in that "moment of communication" where they are in deep rapport, you will notice that a pattern begins to emerge. Their gestures and postures match, that is, they exhibit the same physical characteristics as each other. There is a dance between them: the vocal qualities are the same - volume, pitch, tempo and cadence.

So to put this in practice you would mirror another's body postures and gestures to get into rapport.

Shadowing

Shadowing the person you wish to learn the skill from, in part, enables you to pick up the pattern of their behaviours at an unconscious level and "tune in" your motor skills to theirs. This allows you to develop the necessary motor skills through action, rather than observation. The patterning of these motor skills will assist you in learning unconsciously which parts of the skill to be learnt are important to keep and which aren't. If you attempted to do this consciously, then you could spend a very long time indeed, as our conscious mind is not set up for patterning.

Because people who exhibit excellence in a particular skill do not have the conscious capacity to understand what they do and how they do it, learning in this fashion is like trying to look down a cone-shaped funnel to see the world; naturally you would be missing an enormous amount of information that would otherwise have been available to you if you attended to the world without the funnel.

It is therefore important to model without this funnel (conscious attention) in place. What else can NLP Modelling be used for? In short, anything you desire or wish to learn.

Some examples:

Photographic Memory
Leadership - Visioning
Someone who has the ability to consistently take their vision and make it happen
Motivation
Spelling
Any sporting endeavor

The arts - learn to paint, draw or sculpt
Language skills of politicians
The exceptional healing skills of health practitioners
Those who manage other people very well - the ability to gain trust and respect
Relationships - those who can meet people on the first meeting and entrance them
Retention of information or the ability to understand complex information and make sense of it for others
The possibilities are endless!!

Mark's Modelling Tip

One of my top tips has to be to model a successful practice. Find a successful practice that has similar business vision and philosophy as yours and copy it. Yes it's that simple, find a successful practitioner in the same field as you and copy them. Over half of new businesses fail after just 12 months; this will help ensure you won't be one of them as you are working a proven business model.

You need to model them not only physically, but mentally as well, to get optimum results. Find out what makes them tick and what behaviours and thinking strategies they use every day to assure them of their success.

Most successful practitioners are proud of their practice and achievements and are happy to share some of their success stories.

They won't tell you all of their secrets, by the way, but most of them will help you get started on the right track.

When modelling in this way your priorities are to focus on all the income-driving activities. You will not only need to focus on the physical activities and behaviours of this practitioner, but more importantly on the emotional drivers such as confidence, commitment, enthusiasm and belief - and how he or she attains these skills.

Tripartite meetings - The Power Triangle

In a memorable modelling session Mark did with a client he arranged a tripartite meeting with his client (the new practitioner) and a top performing practitioner working for a national organisation as their leading franchisee.

All three of them arranged to talk on a 30-minute power triad call on Skype. In just 30 minutes they learnt enough to turn Mark's client's business around; she trebled her income over the next three months, doubling her activity in just three days.

It wasn't difficult to see why the woman we were modelling had achieved so much. The level of passion and enthusiasm in her voice was contagious. She said she put her success down to her levels of confidence, belief and passion for her business.

She loved what she did, and failure wasn't an option. She visualised the success of her appointments in the minutes leading up to her client meeting and always visualised the outcome she wanted. She achieved six times the national average in new clients each week and was the top performer nationally.

Mark says: "It was the most important 30 minutes of my client's business life. Her business was never the same again. I will be introducing you to different business enhancing tips throughout this book."

How can I apply modelling in setting up my practice?

Think about the concept of modelling and brainstorm all areas you think it could add value to you setting up in your first clinic.

- Your business location
- New Skills you need to learn

- Effective marketing
- Client processes
- Business set-up
- Business profile and brand
- Charging structure
- Your overall proposition
- Website
- Advertising
- Personal development plan

At this early stage of setting up your first practice you can be looking to model successful practices and practitioners as much as possible.

Embracing a proven business model that works is a great place to start. Why try and re-invent the wheel? The first year of your clinic has to be a success, so find out how others did it.

Modelling success leads to success. That is a proven fact and an integral NLP belief. We will be looking at different modelling techniques and where to apply them throughout this book.

Chapter 3: Budgets

Of all the reasons people share with us about why they decided to become a CAM practitioner, there is always one missing: money.

If everyone we talk to is to be believed, the idea that you can make a good living by being a practitioner is the LAST thing on anyone's mind. You can go through an entire degree course or several specific practitioner training courses (we have!) without money once being mentioned. If you're lucky, you may hear vague talk about "career and employment opportunities", but that's usually as far as it goes.

Indeed for many CAM practitioners, money does seem to be a dirty word. Many, many extremely well- and expensively-educated practitioners feel a little "off" about actually charging clients for what they do. It is the rule in the CAM "business", rather than the exception, to undercharge.

The reasons why people go into practice are usually, in order:

1. You want to help people. You may have experienced some personal challenges earlier in life which you resolved successfully with some professional help from a CAM practitioner and you now want to be that professional help.
2. You may have enjoyed a life in the corporate world, have great people skills and want to put them to good use and work for yourself.
3. You like the idea of giving something back and want to add value to other people's lives in some way, rather than pushing paper round a desk.
4. You want to start your own business and get out of the rat race, learning and getting qualified in

something new and exciting – perhaps you also like the idea of university for a few years.

5. You know someone who has embarked on this journey and it has changed their life to such a degree you want to do something similar.

Now whatever your reason – and no matter how worthy and "right on" it is - earning a living HAS to be up there as a top priority. You won't be able to sustain your practice beyond a few months if you don't earn any money; and then what use are you going to be to anybody?

So it's important you give a lot of thought at this early stage to money, to your potential income. We go further. Now is the time to sit down and decide, specifically, how much you want to earn. How much do you NEED to earn? Come up with an actual figure. Set this as a non-negotiable income target for your business for the first 12 months.

In exactly the same way you need to establish how much money you have to spend on your business. Again, figure this out and set non-negotiable budgets to ensure you manage your expenditure. Failing here could also cause you to go out of business after only a few months.

At this stage, we're not interested in "how" you are going to achieve the income you want, nor whether you think you can afford what you need to spend on the basic set-up. What we're looking for is what you want.

As some of you may have realised, what we've snuck up on you here in the disguise of some enjoyable visioning and planning, is actually a proposed balance sheet, showing income and costs associated with your business. Gasp! This is almost a business plan! And you enjoyed it – admit it!

You now have the fundamentals to begin planning your budget for your first year of trading.

Mark's Modelling Tip

When you start setting up your own practice you need to make sure you have enough savings behind you to act as a capital reserve for the first six months of trading.

If this isn't possible, you are better off starting up part-time and having another part time job while you get your practice off the ground.

It is not a good idea to run your practice on an inadequate budget. We'd advise you to put off your start-up. You will feel under constant financial pressure and your clients will pick up on it.

The only other green light situation is if your total family income is sufficient to meet all of your personal needs during this set-up period and your practice will generate a secondary family income.

• Charging your Clients

Whenever Mark has trained CAM practitioners over the years, there is always a point in the course which provokes a contentious debate. It's the part about charging clients.

It always creates unease. Mark has learnt from experience that this is down to a handful of personal challenges that erupt for practitioners at this early stage of set-up. It is often due to a lack of confidence or belief in their potential value to future clients.

Practitioners often haven't given this a lot of attention as the focus has been on getting into practice and starting to help people towards better health and more fulfilling lives. That's what we all want to be getting on with, but here comes the money thing to bite us. The problem can be chunked down into three key issues:

1. How can I charge for what I do – I'm helping people and it feels wrong?

2. I can't possibly charge that sort of money - people can't afford it.
3. I'm not worth that much money.

Many practitioners struggle with this charging dilemma in the early stages of setting up their own practice. Here's the good news: it will pass. It is often a short-term problem and once your confidence increases the problem becomes far easier to deal with.

Always remember these two key points:

1. You are in business to earn money; without money you have no business
2. The value you put on your services is reflected in your charges. Clients will often be led by this. The cheapest is not always the best. Low rates are not always the best answer.

A sensible approach is to research similar businesses in the area you wish to work in. Couple this with your own experience, especially in the area you are going to work in, and allow your charges to reflect your findings.

Mark's Modelling Tip

Clients will always migrate towards the overall profile and charges of the business. For example, if you decide to target a high net worth client such as a business executive or focus on a high value area, the charge needs to match the potential client – they are not looking for the cheapest option, and if your charges are not high enough they won't take you seriously.

If you target these areas of affluence your charging needs to be at the top end, as this is what this type of client will be looking for and expect.

Practitioners often reduce their prices to get more clients. This is the worst thing they can do and often is reflected in their practice becoming less busy than it was before the price reduction. It's all about the value you put on yourself; the clients will follow.

• Setting your Budget

When setting your first business budget you will have to work with a certain set of assumptions.

If you have done your research and started to model a colleague, you will have an idea of what you can potentially earn in your first year. Equally and as importantly, you will also have, through research, an idea of your potential costs in your first year of trading.

• Managing your Costs

Typically you can split your costs into the following areas:

1. **Fixed costs**
2. **Controllable costs**

   1. Fixed costs represent static costs that rarely change and are often non-negotiable. They include:

      - Room Rental
      - Premises
      - Utility Bills
      - Credit Card Machine
      - Insurance
      - Professional Memberships
      - Data Protection Membership to ICO
      - Website hosting and Domain names
      - Salary

- N I Contributions
- Bookkeeper / Accountant

2 Controllable costs represent other costs that vary and often we have much more control over .They can be referred to as choice costs. They include the following

- Stock
- Office Equipment
- Computers
- Stationery
- Consumables
- Petrol
- Printing and postage
- Promotional Costs
- Leaflets and Posters
- Advertising
- Personal Development and CPD
- Transport

Because of your modelling and research you will be able to calculate fairly accurately what your total running costs are going to be in your first year. You simply list all fixed and controllable costs on a spreadsheet - that will show your first year running costs and it will give you an insight into what you need to aim for in terms of turnover, income and/ or numbers of clients in your first year.

In exactly the same way you will be able to forecast how much income you will be able to deliver based on certain assumptions. This is basic Business Forecasting and is a must for anyone setting up their first clinic or practice. Business Forecasting coupled with intuitive modelling ensures your business every success in that important first year.

Business Forecasting is also a great way to take stock if you are contemplating a re-launch, or if you are one of those practitioners who has kind of stumbled into a fairly enjoyable part-time practice and now want to take things to the next level.

• Business Forecasting

Mark has used this technique in every clinic and business he has ever set up, and he has shared this technique through his coaching sessions that have launched hundreds of new start-up businesses over the years.

"It never fails", he says.

Mark's Modelling Tip

I have used Business Forecasting in many businesses over the years and I have found it adds focus, vision and strategic thinking to your everyday behaviours as a business owner.

You know exactly where you are at any point in any scenario, and some say it invokes another set of rules altogether - known as the Law of Attraction.

Just think for a moment. Every day you wake up knowing exactly what you need to generate as income and exactly how much you need to spend on your business.

What is Business Forecasting?

Business Forecasting is a calculation that involves you forecasting all of your costs in association with running your business. It also allows you to forecast income levels based upon certain assumptions you will have made from your modelling sessions and research.

You should always forecast the first three years of your business to cater for potential growth and potential additions and changes to your proposition each year. You also allow for extra income streams and inflation.

Many successful start-up businesses throughout the UK currently work with a figure of 20%-50% growth year on year. That is an expected and achievable growth figure.

When you complete a business forecast you would do it monthly January to December each year for the first three years of yo9our practice.

Here's an example:

Year 1

Average Clients per Week	= 5
Average Client Fee	£100
Weeks Worked	= 45 (Allowing for holidays)
Products sold nil	
Total Client Income/ Turnover	**= 45 x 5 x £100 = £22,500**

Year 2

Average Clients per Week	= 7
Average Client Fee	£105
Weeks Worked	= 45
Products Sold	= £1500
Total Client Income/ Turnover	**= 45 x 7 x £105 = £33,075 + £1500 = £34,575**

Year 3

Average Clients per Week	= 10
Average Client Fee	£110
Weeks Worked	= 45
Products Sold	= £3000
Total Client Income/ Turnover	**= 45 x 9 x £110 = £44,550 + £3000 = £47,550**

You then need to forecast your fixed and controllable costs and deduct these from this figure to give you your net profit. Costs are easier to forecast as you will eventually have the previous year's information on which to base all of your calculations.

Your three-year business forecast forms part of your overall business plan and gives you an insight and focus on what you can expect to deliver as your net profit.

It is great for building confidence and belief, as the more you see you are achieving in line with your forecast the more action you will take. The more action you take will give you better results and subsequently increase your levels of belief and self confidence. It's a win win situation.

The key is to ensure your forecast is realistic and achievable. You're better off under-forecasting and keeping a tighter control on your costs. It is common to under-forecast and over-deliver in your first year of practice. At least your costs are always kept under control. Never spend what you can't forecast.

Remember: an idea is only an idea until you write it down. Then it becomes a plan. You can work to a plan.

Practitioner Case Study

Putting it into practice: how Mark did it

In my first year of having my own practice my coach told me I could expect to earn at least £50,000-£100,000 in my first year, no problem! I wasn't convinced, and decided to do the numbers myself by doing a forecast

I went away and did a five-year forecast. In year 1 I modelled the best practitioner I could find and did my research.

I calculated in year 1 I would turnover £36,000 with £15,000 worth of costs. I actually turned over £36,039 with £14,899 in costs. This was based on seeing 25 clients a month (6 a week), seasonalised over the year allowing for my activity to increase as I got more established.

In year two I forecast £45,000 with the same cost base as by then I was managing my costs effectively and knew what I could cut down on. I achieved dead on £45,000 and my costs were slightly less than forecast at £13,533. This was based on 33 clients a month (8 a week) and a10% increase in my fees.

In year three I put my prices up in line with my new target market and the new area I was working in. My fees went up by 50%. My forecast was based again on 20% growth on my activity and income and allowing my costs this time to go up by a further 10%. My forecast was £72,000 of income based upon seeing 40 clients a month (10 a week, 2 a day). I came in at the end of the year £3,000 over forecast and my costs were spot on.

• Performance Trends and Hotspots

As you can see, this exercise can be invaluable, as it lets you virtually see in advance what you are going to achieve. On top of that, when you start comparing your performance year on year, you get a great deal of information about trends.

• Seasonalisation

For instance, by studying the year-on-year monthly results, Mark could clearly see which periods of the year were the busiest and which were quiet. He discovered that all of the school holiday periods were very quiet; this seems to be true for most practitioners.

This not only allowed him to plan for those quiet periods and use the time as productively as possible, but it also gave him the idea to of increasing his activity either side of these quiet periods so that his overall annual performance wouldn't be affected and he would meet his forecast. Mark calls this "seasonalisation".

He ended up developing a strategy to manage the quiet periods when other practitioners were often caught unawares and panicked every summer when they had little to do.

Business Forecasting is a must-do exercise, a non-negotiable for the practitioner who wants to be in control of their practice results and success. Set aside a couple of days and complete your three-year forecast based on your research and modelling activities. Remember, if you are modelling correctly you are basing your forecast on a proven business model (someone else's successful practice) and on real costs. This information is the Holy Grail of all business planning. Income and Costs. You have them in advance. Focus on them and you will deliver on your plans. Your forecasting document will form an integral part of your overall business plan, when we talk about planning in the next section.

• Setting up your Accounts

Whether you opt to start as a limited company or simply as a sole trader you will need to adopt a robust accounting process that is water tight and open for inspection by an accountant or the Inland Revenue, if they choose to review and inspect your business.

This accounting system will record and show every item of cost and expense as discussed earlier as well as every pound of income earned.

Now stay with us! Stay on this page and keep reading!

We know that for most practitioners this is not a particularly thrilling subject; in fact it is downright daunting for most. But here's the good news. Two bits of good news, in fact.

1. If you follow the instructions here, your accounts will get completed simply and efficiently; once you get into the habit the whole process will take just a few minutes each month. This is the same system that Mark uses and has taught all his CAM clients.

2. Once you have this organized – and really, it is pretty easy – you will be able to see at a glance how you are doing in terms of income and costs and you will never be surprised by the Inland Revenue, unforeseen bank charges or any other unpleasantness.

You will set this system up to be triggered by the arrival of your business banking statement. All you have to do is make sure you keep all of your receipts from day 1 and that client files mirror the fees logged in the credit side of your accounting statements each month.

You have some choice about whether you do your accounts yourself or employ an accountant or bookkeeper.

Some practitioners employ a bookkeeper for a day or so a week to keep their accounts up to date; some use an accountant. If you are a limited company then you need an accountant.

You will also need to keep a record of all spending in the form of receipts and even keep a log of any business miles if you are claiming mileage for business trips. (The current rate is 40 pence per mile.)

• The Role of your Accountant

The accounts process you will now learn is a simple but robust process that you can manage yourself, saving in bookkeeper's costs. If you are a limited company you will still need to get final sign-off from an accountant, but it will keep their costs to a minimum. (For a sign-off and checking service from an accountant the fee is generally around £300.)

From 2012 certain reports have to be filed online and this can prove to be a bit tricky for the less computer literate among us. These reports include a P35 and P14 for any employees, together with your final end of year tax return that will need to be filed online if you are a limited company. Self-employed practitioners can still file their tax returns by hand and manually. An accountant will charge you around a further £100 for completing any of these returns on your behalf.

Mark' s Modelling Tip

Get a business bank account. Open a business bank account in the name of your business. This is the first step in the simple, effective system you are going to put into practice.

Many banks will offer you free business banking for the first 18 months of trading. These include NatWest, Lloyds and Santander. Check these out and find the bank that meets your needs the most.

All of these banks will offer you free set-up advice and often issue you with a free start-up pack that includes details of their set-up services and templates for business plans and so on. Then arrange to have monthly statements sent to your business address

---

• Accounts Made Simple

After you have set up your bank account, trot down to WH Smith and buy a foolscap folder and an accounts ledger. You are looking for the double entry ledger.

Keep this process as simple as possible; follow the instructions here and you will find yourself the proud owner of a simple but robust accounting system.

The Tax Year

Your trading year will begin when you begin to trade and it is sensible to finish your trading year on 31/3 in line with the UK's end of tax year dates. Your next trading year will then be 1/ 4 to 31/3.

Use your dedicated business account as your own audit trail of fees and expenditure. Put every practice-related expense, payment or income through that account and everything will be shown on your monthly statement from your bank.

As soon as you get that statement, once a month transfer all of these numbers to the ledger you bought. Designate a page for every month and divide each monthly page into two halves. Write the title "Debits" on the left hand side, and "Credits" on the right hand side. Credits will be all of your client income and fees. Debits will be all associated business running costs. Total each column, which will give you a total for debits and a total for credits.

You then deduct all debits from the credits, and that leaves you with a net monthly profit figure each month.

Add up your 12 months at the last month which should be March and you will have a total auditable net profit figure for the year. This provides an auditable trail of all expenses and fees, beginning with your bank account and being accounted for in your accounting ledger. Remember to keep all receipts. Remember, this system is ideal for sole traders and some limited companies, however there are also good computer packages that can be used, such as QuickBooks.

The system explained here is reliable as it is manual and you are in control and aware of every entry, whether it be client fees or costs. It will enable you to keep on top of all business costs and force you to be very close to all of your profit and loss deliverables. The bigger and more established your practice becomes, the more advanced your accounting process will need to be to deal with the increase in fees, costs etc.

VAT

When you reach a turnover of £70,000 you will need to advise the VAT office and you will be liable to pay VAT on top of your charges. The current rate is 20%. This will involve completing a further return and will allow you to claim back certain VAT costs your business has incurred. At that point it is probably time to hire an accountant who can deal with VAT returns for you.

Allowable Expenses

The Inland Revenue will allow you to offset legitimate business expenses against your profits. These expenses must be spent in the course of the day to day functioning of your business. Telephone, office running costs, car mileage are some obvious examples. All costs mentioned earlier under fixed and controllable costs can be offset against profit as expenses.

Accounting paperwork

You should be able to document your monthly accounting schedule from your bank statement, however it is important you refer to and keep the following documentation - for at least seven years - so your accounting system is water tight:

- Bank Statements
- Paying-in Books
- Cheque Books
- Credit Card Statements
- All receipts
- Invoices
- A copy of your appointments diary

Practitioner Case Study

The Importance of Action

When my friend started a scented candle business, it was because she LOVED scented candles. She cared nothing about business theory or how to put it into practice, she just **LOVED** scented candles.

It's easy to fall in to the trap of believing that if *you* love your product or service enough, then everyone else will too; if *you* are passionate then why wouldn't everyone else feel that passion and rush to buy from you?

The reality often crushes that wonderful passion of an enthusiastic new business owner.

I love people, all people and their stories; that's why I wanted to run my own life coaching business. I took my courses, studied hard, read the right books, practised on my friends and finally started my practice. I am passionate about what I do, but one thing from my courses that really stuck was "this is a business", and that no matter how passionate I am, there is more to it than client appointments.

I could see clients all day every day, but where would those clients come from if I wasn't doing more than seeing clients! I need to take action!

The Cycle of Action

1.   Right level of fixed appointments

I was taught that there are three types of action needed to run a small "alternative business" like mine, all equally important, all needing time spent on them. It's like a cycle that must never stop. Firstly, there are my "Fixed Appointments", seeing clients, the thing I love, but that's just one-third of it.

2.   Maintaining your level of fixed appointments

This is about replacing finishing clients with new ones. This concerns revenue-driving activity or "Attracting": all the action we need to take to bring our clients to us; this section is big, really big.

3. Managing your income and client pipeline

Finally our "Pipeline of Money" - this is our invoices, our outstanding revenue, which we need to be on top of and chasing regularly; after all we are not volunteers, this is a business.

Top Tips for managing the Cycle of Action
So, let's focus on Fixed Appointments, this is simple, it's our bread and butter, the reason we went into this business. I learnt some tips to keep this part ticking over,

1. Programmes versus the Session

Firstly "book a programme not a session": every client issue should have a planned programme of sessions. Whether it's for weight loss, stress or relationship problems, sell the programme. It's better to set the client's expectations regarding time and cost and it's better for business.

2. Get the client into your diary before they leave their appointment

If you don't have a programme booked, always book another session with the client before they leave. Don't leave it to the client to prioritise your business - you do it.

3. Maintenance Sessions

Every six months book a maintenance session; this keeps you in touch with the client and reduces the likelihood of them turning to another practitioner...because they live nearer, or know their family, or because they are cheaper or for any other reason.

Tony Curtis famously said, "I can't sit around and wait for the telephone to ring", and neither can we. Tony knew those great roles weren't going to come to him, so he took action and the rest is history.

If we want the telephone to ring (or email and text alerts to sound!) we need to attract our clients to us. No matter how well we are doing, no matter how many fixed appointments we have, we still need to keep the cycle going. Yet it's too easy to become complacent.

So what kind of revenue-driving activity are we talking about? You website and its Google rating will be key to your success.

The website must look professional and will need on-going maintenance and regular updates to keep it interesting.

How about a blog, too? This is great for your website rating and writing on different topics will keep you up to date on your subject knowledge.

Writing for relevant publications, both local and/or national will also demonstrate your knowledge and potential clients will view you as an expert: great for business! "It's who you know not what you know" is kind of true, so contact everyone and anyone you know who may be able to help you increase your client base; it's easier to approach someone you have a link to than someone you don't, so use your personal network.

Workshops are great for creating potential business RIGHT NOW. Running a workshop on an interesting and relevant topic will attract a room full of potential clients, just waiting to hear all about your topic AND your business (remember your business cards!).

Leaflet drops may be more traditional, but they are no less effective, however they must carry a relevant and clear message and be delivered to the right audience.

Building up your own database of clients and potential clients' contact information is very important, and your list should be treated like gold dust. Sending regular newsletters with relevant and interesting updates will interest potential clients and ensure existing clients don't forget you. You may also like to email special offers in your quieter months.

Find potential partners; this can lead to some very useful joint ventures with other practitioners who complement the services you offer, but remember this is a business so all partnerships need to be equal - you have to get something out of it too! You might find networking events useful, you never know who you might meet, and ask around other practitioners for recommendations.

The final part of the puzzle is your pipeline of money. I'm sure, like me, you didn't start your practice planning to ruthlessly chase down payments, but you are providing a professional service and you deserve your money.

One tip I was given was to print out all your outstanding invoices and leave them in your in-tray; this provides a visual reminder of how much money you are owed and can expect over the next month. Always include payment terms on your invoices. Most importantly make it clear how long the client has to pay the invoice, so you have a handle on your cash flow, ie how much available money you have and when.

It is unusual, but as practitioners we will all come across non-payers. It's difficult to find the right approach, but it's important to have an approach. Whether you write a letter, a series of emails or call them direct will all depend on the client and how well you know them, but taking action by creating a plan will make the process so much easier to handle, when it does happen.

Although you may find it hard, spending time on all three of these activities - fixed appointments, attracting clients and your pipeline of money - is sensible and will keep the business cycle going. It is integral to understand that there is more to running a successful business than loving the service or product that you provide; don't sit back, stand up and take action.

Melanie Firth - Wellbeing Coach: www.lifepractice brighton.co.uk

---

Part 2: Achieving a Successful Practice - the first 6 months

Chapter 4: The Business Plan

Mark can't remember the last time he coached a CAM practitioner who had a business plan of any substance. But it's not just us! It's typical of business in general. Even clients who are in business and turn up for business coaching or mentoring rarely if ever have a formal business plan. The same is true of nearly all small and medium sized businesses.

It's not really all that surprising. Business Plan = "Groan!" for most of us. We think of bank managers and accountants. And you'll notice we didn't hit you with this in chapter 1. But wait up: there's something very very interesting about Business Plans. OK, that's a lie. It's the PROCESS of writing a Business Plan that is interesting. The process is potentially inspirational and, dare we say, transformational. Really.

Think on this. The process of coming up with a formal written Business Plan is going to involve a lot of thinking about you, about what precisely you want from your practice, how exactly you want to make a difference in people's lives and what success – however you define it – really means to you. On top of that we'll be asking you to envision where you'll be in one, three and five years from now. Doesn't that sound like fun!

So this antipathy towards Business Plans not only flies in the face of good business practice, but more than that, it's almost even more unexpected from a CAM point of view, as most of us have slightly "alternative" interests and we all "know" the importance of having clear goals and objectives – and the imperative of writing them down. Which is basically what a Business Plan involves (with financial numbers and timescales attached, of course).

You can get as New Age as you like about this, but the fact remains that it has been proved many times over that if you write down what you want to achieve you have a much, much better chance of achieving it – or "attracting" it, if you prefer to put it that way.

A story told many times over is that of the graduating Harvard MBA class of 1979. This research first surfaced in the 1986 book by the world's then top sports agent Mark McCormack, "What They Don't Teach You at Harvard Business School" (Bantam).

In 1979, the year they graduated with their masters degrees in business, researchers asked the students: "Have you set clear, written goals for your future and made plans to accomplish them?" Only 3% had written goals; 13% had goals, but not in writing; and 84% had no specific goals at all. Hm. So much for business school, you might think – and you'd be right, because when they interviewed the graduates ten years later, the differences were astonishing.

The 13% of the class who had goals were earning, on average, twice as much as the 84% who had no goals at all. But wait for it: the 3% with clear written goals were earning, on average, ten times as much as the other 97% put together.

So we're going to be some time on this process. To get you to the point where you can formulate clear written goals AND the action steps to bring them into being. Your Business Plan lesson from the Harvard experience is stark: keeping your ideas in your head, or as random notes scattered all over the place simply doesn't work.

A Business Plan cements the foundations, values and vision of your business; the good news is that if you haven't got one in place at the moment, things will improve dramatically once you do.

• Short, Medium & Long Term Business Planning

Writing a Business Plan is important; writing a meaningful Business Plan that captures the short, medium and long term future of your business is vital.

This often goes overlooked; most business owners focus on just one period – if any at all. We know the attraction: who wants to be tied up with a plan that will dictate our life for the next 3 or 5 years? Many of us think we're doing well if we have a plan for the WEEK.

The thing to get over here – as in "get over" yourself – is the idea that once the plan is in place it cannot change. Not at all. Your plan is flexible. You must be able to adapt as the world of CAM, of business, of health-related legislation changes. As it inevitably will.

With that understood, you will find it easy to commit to forecasting your business results – think of that as dreaming - in line with your short, medium and long term plans. Every plan will include anticipated appointment levels, income levels, activity, your different income streams - and your costs. Here's a breakdown of each plan and what you might include:

1 Short term plan: 6-12 months

- Start-up actions
- Renting of room
- Ordering stationery
- Creating first website
- First attempt at advertising and marketing

2 Medium term plan: 12-36 months

- Ongoing review of Action Plan
- More advanced marketing campaigns
- Joint ventures
- Adding new income streams
- Media marketing
- Personal development
- Adding new therapeutic disciplines
- Formulation of and addition to product range
- Review/change of premises

- Effective change management programme
- Ongoing CPD
- Data marketing
- Business development

3 Long term plan: 36-60 months

- Effective change management program
- A review of short and medium term business plans
- A more strategic view of your overall business proposition
- Merging or acquiring new businesses
- Product development
- Keeping up with economic and legislative change
- Attainment of further qualifications
- Ongoing CPD
- Strategic business development

The lists can go on and on.

Mark's Modelling Tip

A successful practitioner has 1 Business Plan that includes short, medium and long term actions. This is how you keep on top of your growing practice, manage change and stay ahead of the competition.

It may look like we're asking you to produce three plans. No – there is One Plan, and One Plan to rule them all...

You simply include short, medium and long term actions in the same plan and review the plan every month. The key is to dedicate your time using the following time weightings

Short term plan	70%
Medium term plan	20%
Long term plan	10%

● Philosophy, Vision & Mission

What does your practice represent to you and, most, importantly the outside world?

The set-up stage of any business involves a lot of thought and reasoning. This is the point where you examine your business philosophy, vision and mission. All three of these are integral to any business plan or goal-setting exercise.

1. **Philosophy** – literally "the study of any particular proposition such as those connected with existence, knowledge, values, reason and language".

So what are you really about as a CAM practitioner? Why do you do what you do? What do you and your business truly stand for?

As an exercise, write a statement announcing your business identity and philosophy; you are making it public for the first time simply by writing it down.

This statement should represent your feelings, thoughts and rationale for your business, focusing on your fundamental business values.

Vision - while any business needs to constantly change to meet external environmental challenges such as competition etc there are certain core business ideals that remain constant and unchanged. These ideals form the business vision and are expressed in the business mission statement. Where are you going? Where do you see yourself in 1, 3 or 5 years' time – or even farther out? In what way do you want to change the world?

Mission Statement - your business mission statement communicates to the public your practice ethos, core values and business goals or identity. It is informed by your philosophy and vision. It's where it all comes together in a concise way.

Yes, "mission statement". Business jargon. You're right to shy away from it. But please stay and play with it; the core success strategies of any business are the same. Just because you are not (yet?) a big international company and maybe never want to be, doesn't mean you can't use the tools that have been proven to work.

It's vital to not only write down your practice mission statement but also eventually to publish it on your website, stationery, even on the wall of your clinic or place of work. Be proud of what your practice stands for and your clients will feel the same way.

"A company can function without a vision statement, but it cannot operate without a mission statement", as they say.

When writing a mission statement you should start with:

1. Your Purpose
2. Your Process
3. Your values
4. Your goals

Ideally you want a minimum of three of each when formulating your practice ethos and identity.

Purpose

- Direction you want to take your practice
- Why you formed your practice
- What your practice will do for your clients

Process

- How you will operate
- Logistics and location
- Methods of communication

Values

- First-class customer service
- Integrity and professionalism
- Value-adding services

Practice Goals

- The short, medium and long term practice plans
- To become the best at what you do
- To achieve sales and income targets

Ensure your goals follow the **CSMART** principles of goal-setting. This will make sure you set realistic and achievable goals for your practice. There's nothing worse than setting goals with no chance of achieving them. As Functional Medicine "guru" Dr Jeff Bland told a class that Simon was attending 30 years ago (and yes, he still remembers it): "Achievable goals lead to a stress-free life!"

CSMART stands for **C**ommitment, **S**pecific Goals, **M**easurable, **R**ealistic, **T**imescales.

More about this later on. Once you have that all clear in your head, then cook it all down to a simple powerful statement that won't take half an hour for clients to read!

As an example of a mission statement, here's one from nutritional therapist Karen Webb: "The aim of Neuro Nutrition is to provide first-class nutritional advice combined with quality products and services at competitive prices, to provide value for money for all our customers".

Here's the mission statement of Debbie Best of www.best-nutrition.co.uk : "At Best Nutrition our aim is to provide you with the right nutritional advice specifically for your needs and to empower you on your journey to improved health and wellbeing."

Another nutritional therapist, Renate Larkin, Dip ION, mBANT, puts it this way on her Edible Health site (www. edible-health.co.uk): "During a one to one consultation, we will agree on a nutritional strategy that will help you achieve what you want to achieve.

"What we won't do is set unrealistic goals that you can't maintain. We will monitor your progress with as many follow-ups as you feel you need, until you are ready to take control yourself."

And speaking of Jeff Bland, what about the mission statement for his Institute for Functional Medicine (www. functionalmedicine.org). This is worth looking at as an example of a well-defined, public statement of what the IFM is about and how it is going to achieve its goals – from an organization that is successfully changing the way in which medicine is practised. The IFM website not only has a clear mission statement, but also a vision/strategic plan explaining how it is going to achieve its objectives. Very nice.

"The mission of The Institute for Functional Medicine is to serve the highest expression of individual health through widespread adoption of functional medicine as the standard of care.

"The main objective of The Institute for Functional Medicine is to reverse today's epidemic of chronic disease through education, research, and collaboration. Functional medicine provides a powerful new operating system and systems-based clinical model to replace the outdated and ineffective acute-care models carried forward from the 20th century. It enables physicians and other health professionals to practice proactive, predictive, personalized medicine and empowers patients to take an active role in their own health."

And finally, here's one from a very well-known and highly successful business. Guess who: "Our mission: to inspire and nurture the human spirit – one person, one cup and one neighbourhood at a time."

Yes, that's Starbucks!

So, jump past the jargon and keep it simple. Brainstorm and write down your practice philosophy, your vision and the objectives and goals for your practice. Cook that down to your mission statement. This process is immensely inspiring and rewarding. And there's a sneaky bonus. While you're having fun with it, you are actually laying the foundations of your first business plan – without even realising it!

• The Power SWOT

The next phase of your planning stage is to complete a SWOT analysis.
SWOT stands for **S**trengths, **W**eaknesses, **O**pportunities, **T**hreats.

It's a great tool to help you review and evaluate many different business scenarios. You can use it to evaluate and help you decide the best course of action in many different areas. For example:

- Business set up analysis and action
- Competitor analysis
- Marketing ideas
- Budget decisions
- Business planning
- Business partnerships
- Strategic planning
- Business development
- Choosing a product supplier
- Investment opportunities
- Business partnerships
- CPD opportunities and further training

Because SWOT enables you to gather, investigate and review information and look at the results objectively, it can really help you write a Business Plan that accurately represents your current situation.

We talked in section 1 about the research business model SLEPT. The important difference to understand is that SWOT measures an idea whereas SLEPT measures a market.

When does a SWOT become a Power SWOT? When used in business planning, due to the power, focus and vision it brings to your initial decision making.

Here's the basic SWOT template:

STRENGTHS	WEAKNESSES
OPPORTUNITIES	**THREATS**

And this is what it looks like when we've filled it in:

STRENGTHS	WEAKNESSES
Staff Competence	Gaps in staff competence
Unique selling points	Gaps in proposition
Level of staff experience and knowledge	Lack of staff experience and knowledge
Staff commitment	High staff attrition
Capability of resource	Poor financials and cash flow
Cash flow	Uncompetitive costs
Low costs	Poor location affecting walk-byand regular trade
Business logistics and geographics	Uncompetitive qualification
Qualifications	
OPPORTUNITIES	**THREATS**
New markets	Competition
Unique proposition	Political and legislative changes
Market demands	Environmental effects
Global influences	Market demands
Modelling a proven model	Economy home and abroad
Legislation and market trends	Reliability of business partners

Now to see how a new practitioner's first Power SWOT might look, follow this case study.

Mel has been fully qualified as a nutritional therapist for ten years. She has worked successfully for all that time renting a room from her local GP and has had a steady stream of GP referrals throughout that time.

She pays 20% of her fees to rent her room in the surgery.

Her earnings are in line with her goals and she really enjoys working at the GP's surgery as she gets to mix with the staff every day and loves feeling part of the team. Despite being happy and successful she feels she needs new challenges and wants to take her business to a new level. She wants to open her own clinic in the same town and hopes to take on an assistant within the first 12 months to help with her administration, as she has never enjoyed that side of the business.

At the GP's surgery she sees on average ten clients per week over three days, however she now believes she can see more clients and has set her goals at 15 clients per week, working five days and increasing her earnings by 50%.

She has a small daughter at primary school and the school has agreed her daughter can attend after school club until 6pm.

The whole new idea excites Mel and she is sure she will be a huge success. She is sad at leaving the GP's surgery but aims to keep in touch by meeting up for a coffee once a month. Before making a firm decision Mel decided to complete a Power SWOT to help her make the right decision:

STRENGTHS	WEAKNESSES
Ten years' experience	New Location = extra responsibility
Known in town	Rent, rates, bills extra costs
Good reputation	Working alone to start with
Highly qualified	No more referrals from GP
Committed and enthusiastic	New relationships
Should keep regular clients	New clients
Potential 50% increased income	Longer hours
Personal fulfillment	Has to reinvent self
Proven track record	

OPPORTUNITIES	THREATS
Learn new skills in business management	Competition
Logistics and geographics of practice	Lack of clients
Attract more clients	Logistical and geographical costs and financial implications
Will be in full control	No income stability
Potential to earn more money	Challenge of working alone
Be more successful	No longer part of a team
Create new cross-functional business relationships	Legal and economic impact
Take on staff	Will lose GP referrals
Invest in new ideas	Will lose kudos and credibility of being linked with GP
Potential for further future expansion	Lose preferential room rental terms

After completing the Power SWOT Mel decided she wasn't quite ready to cut loose from the GP surgery. She opted to stay put for another six months and then review the situation. In that time she would start working on attracting clients from other sources, if necessary renting space unused by a CAM colleague in the town.

Complete a POWER SWOT on your own practice, whether you are established or just starting out. See what you learn and what things stand out that maybe you should be doing differently. Write those observations down. This naturally gets you thinking about your business aims and objectives, which leads nicely into writing your Business Plan.

• The Business Plan

Your next step after completing the Power SWOT is to look at the Aims and Objectives of your business. The core part of your Business Plan will address the threats and weaknesses and develop the strengths and opportunities derived from the SWOT.

The complete Business Planning process in its correct order sequence looks like this:

1. Business Forecasting (short, medium and long term)
2. Business Philosophy
3. Business Vision and Mission
4. The Power SWOT
5. Business Aims and Objectives
6. Business Goals
7. Business Actions
8. Business Plan Review Process - GROW

• Business Aims & Objectives

The Business aims and objectives address the core findings from the SWOT analysis. They will obviously be different in each stage of the short, medium and long term stages of your plan. Brainstorm all of your aims and objectives and then prioritise them in list of importance to you.

Business Goals

Select the 12 highest priority short term objectives and write them down in the form of goals. Always begin by focusing on short term priority objectives and goals followed by subsequent actions.

When establishing goals for our practice we are effectively looking at the "what" we would like to achieve, not the "how". An example of some business goals would be (for a practice looking to set up in 2013):

- My goal is to find suitable practice premises by 1/1/2013
- I want to have conducted the relevant market research by 1/11/2012
- I need to ensure my website is created and in the top 5 of Google by 1/3/2013
- I want all my business stationery to be produced and ready for use with clients by 1/11/2012
- I want to achieve a turnover of £20,000 in my first year of practice
- I want to have secured three cross-functional business relationships by 1/3/2013
- I want to see ten clients a week

• CSMART

The process we use to qualify and validate our goals is CSMART. It stands for:
Commitment, **S**pecific, **M**easurable, **R**ealistic, **T**imescales.

Measuring each goal against CSMART is very valuable – it will quickly tell you whether you've done enough work on your goal.

If you look at the above goals and apply CSMART, how many do you think meet its criteria?

Three of the most important factors in any goal-setting exercise are

1. You review the goals regularly, usually a minimum of monthly.
2. You follow through with actions once you have set your goals.
3. You are flexible with your goal-setting and review and change the goals as and when appropriate.

The model we use to review our goals is called GROW. It stands for

G	The goal itself
R	Reality of achieving that goal
O	Options at review
W	Agree a sensible way forward re planning if necessary.

• The Action Plan

With our goals in place (the "what"), we move on to the "how" and generate an action plan.

This sets out, in detail, the actions you need to take in order to achieve your business goals. Those goals have been formulated through a pretty extensive process of Deep Thought and reflection as you have jogged down the inspiring path of putting words to your business vision, philosophy and mission, and have THEN been objectively researched and examined via your Power SWOT. So by now you're certain these are things you really do want to pursue.

Your action plan "simply" consists of a number of written actions that, again, comply with the CSMART principle. It is simple but it doesn't always start that way. Many of us come up with Big Goals that, when it comes to taking action, can be so big as to be overwhelming. The trick here is to chunk down to a much more detailed level: you can produce as many small action steps as you need – and true to the Jeff Bland principle, this will not only cause less stress, but produce a series of small victories that will build momentum. So feel free to include everything you need to do to achieve your goal and to start with small steps.

Mark's Modelling Tip

When completing an action plan focus on the Top Five goals first.

Anything more than this can distract you from your priorities and can prove overwhelming.

As an example, here is an actual action plan produced by a Life Practice UK associate practitioner while she was in the process of setting up her first clinic.

This was her first attempt at an action plan and you will notice all action dates were set on the same day – actually while she was in the middle of one of Mark's Clinic Builder course. It is a great idea to put a whole day by for this exercise and take yourself off to a supportive environment where you won't be distracted. This action plan evolved as things started to progress. This "action planner" now runs a successful practice in the Channel Islands.

Action Plan 2012

Date	Action	Activity	By When	Who	Update	Closed
2/2	Create website for new practice	Finalise 3/2 go live 1	1/3	john		
2/2	Print leaflets and distribute around area	Vistaprint	1/3	j		
2/2	Obtain Car Banner and fit	Vistaprint	1/3	j		
2/2	Credit card machine	Card save 0844 209150	1/3	j		
2/2	Bus. cards printed	Logo from bob	1/3	M		
2/2	Premises Found, ideally two premises	Aim 2 clinics 1 with a medical connection potential gym	1/4	j		

2/2	Launch Gastro Band initiative	Put together a program and market Life practice balls and mat. Mark to send an example program john to put program together send manual to mark	1/6	M/j	
2/2	Local radio get on local radio as an expert	Local radio presence	1/6	M/j	
2/2	Ensure insurance in place	Applications to complete and send Mark to script	1/3	j	Insured
2/2	Filing cabinet	Purchase	1/4	j	done
2/2	logo	Await from bob,	1/3	M	
2/2	Logo forms	Await from bob,	1/3		

Date	Action	Activity	By When	Who	Update	Closed
2/2	Joint ventures Find 5 potential business partners	Ongoing Football clubs sports hypnosis	1/6	j		
2/2	earnings	Charge = 12 appts per month 144 appts per year				
2/2	Investigate Google AdWords Advertising	Google advertising	1/3			
2/2	Audios	Investigate cd production audacity				
2/2	Licence & name	sole trader	1/4			
2/2	Website optim isation to get into top 5 of Google	Finalise website optimisation	1/6			

Writing your Business Plan

Keep it simple but focused. Write it before you go into practice, or certainly before you open your own clinic. If you are already in practice and thinking "I haven't got one of these" - it's never too late.

When to do the Plan

Most of the time. procrastination is a bad thing, but on the other hand, timing is everything! Writing the Plan is inspirational. Wait for the right moment to put it together. When you are feeling creative, resourceful, passionate, and motivated by your business – that's the time to let all your great ideas flow and help form your Business Plan.

What to include

So, one more time: include your philosophy, identity and vision together with your Power SWOT, which is simply an objective, high altitude eagle's eye view of your practice and business set-up, identifying potential strengths, weaknesses, opportunities and threats. As you put it all together, allow your USP – your Unique Selling Point – to emerge. This is what makes your practice different and special.

After completing the SWOT you will have a list of aims and objectives for your practice. From there you move on to list and prioritise your business goals.

Make sure they are CSMART: that there is a firm commitment from you and that they are specific, measurable, achievable, and realistic – and have timescales. Prioritise your top 5 goals – just 5, to avoid overwhelm – to work on and list a series of action steps, which detail how you are going to get what you want.

Remember that your Business Plan must deal with the short, medium, and long term future of your business. Typically 1, 3 and 5 years.

Commit to forecasting your business results for all three periods. Include anticipated appointment levels, income levels, activity, your different income streams and costs.

From then on your Business Plan becomes your blueprint for success. It is personalised and detailed. You know at a glance where you are headed and how well you are doing along the way. Every month sit yourself down – with your partner, advisors or team if you have them – and review your plan using the GROW model... what was the Goal, what is current Reality (ie what is actually happening in your business), what are your Options and what is your Agreed way forward? Redraw the plan if you need to. It's not set in stone.

Be flexible and don't be afraid to reset your goals to more realistic levels if you find yourself struggling. It is far better to achieve a little improvement, a bit at a time than to fail with unachievable goals.

This plan will evolve as things change and it will enable you to be in the position of you driving your business rather than having your business drive you. That is no fun.

Chapter 5: Marketing Your Practice

Your website is one of the most important parts of your business; you have to get right from day one. In fact, it is probably the single most important part of your business; getting it right could be the difference between success and failure.

• Why your website is key

We know that's quite a claim. But think about it.

- 97% of Internet users search for local businesses online (Google)

- 70% of online searches lead to action within one month (Mobile Marketer)

- 63% of people use the Internet as their first resource when looking for a local service or product (Vistaprint)

- 75% of Internet users said they purchased something online (Plunkett Research, Ltd)

- Of 3,000 people surveyed, 47% said they are more likely to purchase services or products from a small business with a website (Discover Small Business Watch Survey)

A final stat from Mark: "I've been on national TV, had my own BBC radio slot appearing monthly as an expert, written a monthly column for five magazines and still 95% of my clients and now students find me online."

Let's take a moment to think about what your website means to you and perspective clients:

- It embraces and shows to the world your business vision, philosophy, ethos, and values
- It is a true representation of who you are and what you provide to potential clients all over the world
- It is your main advertising vehicle, with 75-97% of people now admitting their preferred search and buy tool is the worldwide web

Mark's Modelling Tip

No matter how small a business you are, if you think you can manage without a website you are wrong. If you want to see clients and make money, that is.

Maybe you think the whole thing's too complicated and a step too far; it can wait until later. It can't. Do it now.

A good website will be the difference between you succeeding and failing.

Key website phrases

We talked earlier about different website options and the basic set up process. Now we are going to go into more detail so that you will know how to get the most out of your site. Let's now look at a number of key website phrases you are going to come across and explain what they mean.

1. **Email address**
   Yes, you know what that is, but what we want you to do is to have a separate, business email that reflects your professional practice. When you set up your

practice website you will be given the option of having an address like you@yourwebsite.

2. **Domain Name**
   Your website address and identification

3. **Website host**
   A web hosting service provides space on a server to "park" your website and maintains access 24/7/365.

4. **Keywords**
   The words most commonly used in search engines like Google, Yahoo and Bing by potential clients looking for your services. Often a combination of therapy and a place name. These words need to be on your website.

5. **SEO**
   Stands for Search Engine Optimisation, which is the process of optimising your website so that as many potential clients as possible can quickly find it.

6. **Google AdWords**
   A method to run proactive marketing campaigns on Google, by sponsoring certain keywords and agreeing to pay a certain amount of money for every potential client who clicks through from the ad to your site.

7. **Social Media**
   Sites like Facebook, Twitter and LinkedIn, which can help you inform potential clients that you are in practice – and keep them interested in and educated about what you do.

8. **Website optimisation companies**
   Specialise in raising the profile of your website so that you will come out at or near the top of search results.

Mark's Modelling Tip

Two of this, Two of that, Two of the Other. Or in words you can understand: on your home page mention TWICE

- What you do
- What you offer
- Where you are

• Getting the most from your website

Think of your website as a tool to attract potential clients and encourage them to begin a friendly relationship with you that may last years.

It is the number one tool you need to maintain a constant stream of appointments. Most practitioners really don't like to think of themselves as sales people, but in effect you are in a selling business. You are "selling" yourself and your therapy. Focusing on "sales" – or in our case on getting your appointments diary filled - is more important than anything else, because if you don't have an acceptable income you won't have a business, you won't be in practice and you won't be able to use your training to help and heal.

The facts speak for themselves. Well over 50% of practitioners who graduate with their desired qualifications don't even make the business start-up stage or fail within the first three years. This is much higher than the average for all businesses. The vast majority of CAM course graduates never progress beyond the "friends and family" stage.

This tells you a lot about the typical mentality of those of us entering the "helping" professions. We'll explore this in detail – well actually, we'll keep banging on about it - later on. For now, we just need you to accept the commercial focus required for a successful practice. As you've got this far, you probably are beginning to really "get" that, so all we need to emphasise is there is one thing apart from your personal qualities and specialist knowledge that could possibly guarantee that your practice is successful, it's your website.

The Top Ten Tips to make your website work

We'll assume you have your embryonic website up and running. Now work your way through these ten action steps, one day at a time and at the end of ten days your website will be humming.

As you start working through this section, make sure you read Simon's take on what you are "allowed" to say. The Advertising Standards Authority regards your website as an advertisement. In fact all your practice material – brochures, posters, hand-outs, whatever – is seen as sales material. The way the ASA deals with CAM practices is, in our opinion, unnecessarily heavy-handed, and because it refuses to allow input from CAM experts, is bordering on censorship. It is becoming increasingly difficult to even be "allowed" to explain what your therapy does (unless you have a pile of double-blind, placebo-controlled studies to submit as evidence). More on that later.

In this section we're basing some of our recommendations on material provided with permission by online marketing expert Graham Collingwood (www.thetoppageguru.com). Farther down the line, he's the man to see about getting your site really optimized.

Tip 1 – Make this one change and double your online response

You can break down your Internet marketing and consequent enquiries and new bookings into two distinct steps:

1. **Getting visitors to your site**
2. **Converting them into paying clients**

So how do you double your online response? The answer might appear too simple to be true, but it's not. It's this: rather than trying to sell something right off the page, set up your site so that your visitor is happy to give you their name and email address, so you can "market" to them – from a CAM point of view make this "educate and inform" - over time.

In short, switch from a sales model to a lead generation and contact model. When someone hits your site, your sole intention should be to get them to give you their email address and permission for you to send them your email newsletter (or e-newsletter). No spamming allowed, ever: you MUST get permission.

How do you get them to agree to this? A good way of starting any relationship is by giving them something free. Free articles, CDs and Health Tips all work extremely well. So begin the business relationship by giving. Offer a free report or a free sample or something else that's both valuable and useful to your visitor in exchange for permission to add them to your e-newsletter database.

This should also get you over the "selling" phobia. Yes, you could see the ultimate aim of your website as being to advertise and sell your services – and the Advertising Standards Authority will treat you that way. But really what it's about is building a relationship with people; seeking the opportunity to explain what your practice, your therapy, is about. We're not trying to sell them things like roofing and guttering; we want to teach them about CAM, about the potential benefits of eating right, of working on their health to possibly prevent illnesses and disease and to live longer, more vital and more fulfilling lives. To enable them to do that you have to find out about them and let them find out about you and what you may have to offer. You can only do this by building relationships. To start this process, you need their email and you need them to say yes, they'd like to hear more from you.

Tip 2 - Understand Google Analytics

Google Analytics is a free tool produced and supplied by Google to help you understand visitor activity to your site.

It will tell you

- how many visitors find your site
- how many potential clients visit your site in any given period
- what pages they click on
- what words and phrases they used to find you
- what search engine they used to find you or
- whether they clicked on an ad or a link from another site
- how long they spend on your site and what is the last page they see before they leave

This is all great information that will help you tweak your site; checking these stats will tell you how well or how poorly the words and phrases on your website are working. Your goal is have on your home page key phrases that are generating sales and enquires.

Get along to www.google.com/analytics to get started.

Tip 3 - Increasing serious visitors to your website

On average, only 1% of visitors to a typical website buy anything from that website. For many businesses, the figure is even less. This means that if your website is typical, 99% of your visitors will leave without doing business with you.

That would be a tragic waste of the time, effort, energy and resources you've invested to build your website and your online presence. So here's a checklist to go over with your web designer to make sure you are maximising the most basic opportunities your website presents.

1. Does the home page of your website clearly describe what you have to offer, what you are about, before users have to scroll down the page?

2. Is the first thing that greets visitors a large company logo or a picture? This is a waste of valuable space and not SEO friendly.

3. Are you offering visitors a compelling reason to give you their name and email address when they arrive at your site?

4. Have you tested pay per click advertising - Google AdWords – to drive more already-slightly-interested visitors to your site?

5. Are you successfully using video throughout your site?

6. Is your copy throughout the website all about you, or is it – as it should be – about your visitor's needs, problems and frustrations?
   Remember: "People don't look for credentials, they look for a solution" - James Doulgeris, Senior Strategist, Health Care, HCP.

7. Do you send regular emails to your existing customers and prospective customers?

8. Is your website focused: are you talking directly to your ideal client?

Making your website work is what this is all about. They say in business "fail fast", which means if something's not working, try something else. Keep ringing the changes until you find something that DOES work. So if the any of the above sets your alarm bells ringing, then make the changes. The difference it will make will astound you.

Tip 4 - Push your site to the top of the rankings

Quality scoring is Google's reward and ranking system for your website. If you get a high quality score it will help your overall ranking. If you have a poor quality score you will find your position dropping down the Google charts and rankings. That could mean the difference between appearing on the first page of a Google search result, or the tenth, where potential clients are unlikely to see you.

Why is that important and why do we keep mentioning Google? James Doulgeris is Senior Strategist, Health Care, at HCP, a national research, strategy and marketing firm headquartered in Tampa, Florida (http://hcpassociates. com). He explains:

"People don't look for credentials, they look for a solution, and their search is easier than ever. Eight of ten people do their health care research using the Internet, the vast majority using Google.

"They also post their experiences with providers, good and bad, and they are all just a search phrase away. Search engine rankings not only make your practice more visible, higher rankings have a profound effect on how prospective patients view your capabilities, status and popularity as a provider. Further, your website must be changed from an electronic brochure to an interactive, integrated element of your operation. Websites are no longer mere marketing vehicles; they are a primary service delivery point and are integral to the quality of service and care."

How exactly to get a good quality score is one of Google's best-kept secrets. However, experience shows that it will help your score to keep your website as "clean" – ie simple and minimalistic - and as fair as it can possibly be. Do not make outlandish claims; do not link out to other websites without thoroughly examining them. Stay professional and evidence-based.

Think of it as an auditing exercise: to pass you have to be whiter than white in following Google's audit processes.

Ways towards a high Google quality score

- 90% of Website Optimisation is done on the Home Page.

- Key words describing your services, location, and products must be shown on the home page.
- Google prefer the right balance of Keywords and Phrases
- Look to include two mentions of your keywords focusing on location and services twice each on your home page.
- Don't overuse your Keywords on the home page as it will have a detrimental affect on your Google quality score and affect your overall position on Google. That means don't mention your location and therapy ten times in nonsensical statements – some people do that.
- Google ranking positions take into consideration how long your website has been up and how many visits it gets.

To improve your chances and keep up with Google's ever-changing requirements, it's a good idea to regularly review your site. This enables you to try out different ideas and find out what works to keep a top ranking on Google. Review your website every week.

Tip 5 - Use testimonials

Testimonials are one of the most powerful marketing tools you'll ever have at your disposal. It's easy to say great things about yourself on your website, anyone can do that. But with a testimonial, you've got someone else doing it. And bear in mind this is someone else the reader can identify with, simply because the client in your testimonial is talking about a successful solution to the very problem that has brought the visitor to your site.

One big advantage of having a website is the choice of media you have. You can have video as well as written testimonials. People love to see videos! This is no big surprise, because video is the next best thing to actually being face-to-face with someone.

Getting testimonials doesn't have to be difficult. I always make it part of my process at the end of my time with a client or student to ask them for written feedback on how they found their time with me. I always explain that we are continually looking to improve our client experience and to do that I need their written feedback on how they found my service. I always get written permission to publish their testimonial on my website and to be able to state their real name. High-profile testimonials are very valuable and promote credibility.

Again, keep the presentation of testimonials low-key, simple and professional. No big bells and whistles and ask your clients NOT to claim on your behalf that you have "cured" them or that you achieve miracles! For example, they cannot say you cured them of asthma, even if you did, UNLESS you can produce a copy of a double-blind, placebo-controlled study showing that the treatment you used has been "proven" to cure it. You will probably also need a documented case history and a statement from their GP saying that yes, they did indeed have asthma before you got hold of them.

Instead, get them focusing on the "client experience". They can say how professional, knowledgeable and effective you are, for example. They can (probably) make general statements about how much better they feel, how relieved they were to have found someone to take them seriously and get to the root cause of their problem, and so on. Practitioners are often afraid to ask for a testimonial in the first place or they don't ask to use the client's real name or get permission to say what the treatment was for. The way round this is to just include it routinely and in a matter-of-fact way as part of your routine with clients, from the very start of your practice.

Tip 6 - Use a guarantee

Using a guarantee can increase your enquiry flow by 30%. Mark always insists that practitioners he personally works with must include a strong guarantee. He says: "In all the years I've been promoting this strategy, I've never - never - seen more than a handful of customers take advantage of a guarantee".

One of his business clients was running small website. Just by adding a guarantee to the site, she increased her sales overnight by 37%. The number of people who took her up on the guarantee and wanted their money back? Less than 1%.

A guarantee is known as a "Risk Reversal" technique in business jargon, and for once that accurately describes what's going on. When potential clients are looking for a suitable practitioner they are often anxious and nervous. They're not only stepping into the unknown when they contact you, but this might also be their first experience of CAM, and they're not fully sure about that, either. Any fear or anxiety that they might be about to waste their money will stop them contacting you.

Providing professional reassurance in the form of a product or service guarantee removes that element of fear and shows the potential client that you are confident, that you believe in what you do and that you stand by your results.

As CAM practitioners we cannot guarantee results when we don't know what we might be dealing with. We can't guarantee to cure ANYTHING, let alone any recognised medical conditions. As things stand with the Advertising Standards Authority we are barely able to describe the proven benefits of what we do. However, we CAN guarantee that we will give a client a refund if he or she is not satisfied with our efforts.

Use clear, simple language so there is no confusion about what you are offering. We love the guarantee written by an acquaintance of Simon's in Colorado, Dr Stephen Kaufman,

DC, a chiropractor who runs workshops and sells DVDs about his Pain Neutralization Techniques™ (www. painneutralization.com). This is Stephen's guarantee: "Although most of the practitioners using these techniques are ecstatic about the results, including DCs, L.Acs, MDs etc, YOU won't know until you try them how they'll work for you. Therefore we offer a 30-day, no questions asked, no hassles, you don't need a note from your mother, 100% satisfaction assurance promise. I ABSOLUTELY 100% ASSURE you you'll be thrilled with this material, your patients will jump up and hug you, your practice will grow from referrals, or you pay NOTHING!"

Guarantees are powerful. They can help convince, motivate and encourage a visitor to your website to become a lifetime customer. Put guarantees everywhere on your website.

Mark's Modelling Tip

If you want to be successful and attract lots of clients through your website you have to be in the top five on page one of any relevant Google search result. You must really focus on doing what it takes to make this happen. Nothing else will so easily give you the clients you need to make your practice successful.

Tip 7 - Use influential words

Just as there are certain words that can attract potential clients to your site, so it is that certain words have a stronger influence than others on your potential client when it comes to encouraging them to book your services.

Dawn Josephson, the Master Writing Coach™, has identified 21 Words that Sell. Here she highlights the top ten on her list. Get them on your home page!

1. You/your – "You" is the most powerful word in the English language. It's more powerful than the word "money;" it's more powerful than the word "sex." Prospects want to feel as if you're talking to them directly, and the word "you" accomplishes just that. So instead of writing "health and wellbeing", write "your health and wellbeing". Keep every sentence in your prospect's perspective.

2. Money – Ask people what they wish they had more of, and chances are they'll say "money". People love to save money just as much as the love to earn it. So if your clients can save money in any way by coming to see you – tell them.

3. Health/healthy – The second thing people wish they had more of is good health. People want products and services that are going to either improve their health or not negatively impact it. You cannot make any unproven claims that what you do will improve your client's health, but you must use the word!

4. Guarantee/guaranteed – This one we've covered.

5. Easy/easily – Between 40+ hour workweeks and increasing demands at home, people want things that are easy. They don't want products or services that are going to make their life more difficult. So always state how easy it is to work with you. For example: "Our personalised plans make it easy to get the new habit of eating the foods that are right for you".

6. Free – Everyone loves getting something for nothing. That's why the word "free" continues to be one of the top-selling words of all time. Realise that the free offer doesn't have to have a high monetary value, just a high perceived value. Some freebies that work include: "Free consultation," "Free report", and so on.

7. Yes – Face it, you love being told "yes", don't you? "Yes" means you have permission, you were right, or

you can get what you want. "Yes" is one of the most pleasing words to the human ear.

8. Quick/quickly – In today's microwave age society, people want things quickly. They don't want to wait weeks or even days for the results you promote. They want to know they'll see a quick return for their investment now. This is difficult for us, as we often need to work with people long-term. However, identify a part of your practice protocol that does give quick results.

9. Benefit – Most written marketing pieces do state the benefit of the product or service; however, they neglect to actually use the word "benefit." When people read the word "benefit," they subconsciously perk up. They know they're about to learn something that will impact their life, so they want to know more. For example, "As an added benefit to working with me you will (state the benefit)."

10. Person's name – People love to hear the sound of their own name and they love to read their name in print. Use this idea when you reply to enquiries by email.

The remaining 11

Mix and match using the other eleven words that Dawn has identified. These are: 1) Love, 2) Results*, 3) Safe/safely, 4) Proven*, 5) Fun, 6) New, 7) Save, 8) Now, 9) How-to, 10) Solution* and 11) More.

* Be careful how you use these marked words: you cannot make unproven claims – and the standard of proof the ASA works to is a double-blind, placebo-controlled trial.

Dawn adds: "While synonyms (words with the same meaning) to these 21 words are acceptable, synonyms are not as powerful as the actual word itself. So in order to not appear redundant in what you're writing, use the appropriate word wisely, and don't overdo it.

"As your marketing writing prowess increases, consider combining words that sell in the same sentence. For example, maybe people find a consultation with you "easy and fun". You get the idea. Since short pieces are more powerful than long ones, make sure every sentence packs a punch.

"Can you do it? Yes! And you're going to love the results. Guaranteed!"

(Dawn Josephson, the Master Writing Coach™, is a Writing Coach, Ghostwriter, Editor, Workshop Facilitator, Speaker, and Author. When you get stuck and need some more writing advice check out her information-packed articles on her website: www.masterwritingcoach.com)

No claims, no cures: dealing with the ASA

You may well know a CAM practitioner who has received a threatening letter from the Advertising Standards Authority. When the ASA expanded its remit in March 2011 to cover digital media, a campaign organised by an anti-CAM group led to nearly 800 practitioners being told they had breached the British Code of Advertising, Sales Promotion and Direct Marketing (The CAP code).

Jayney Goddard, president of the Complementary Medical Association, said: "We have asked our members how they feel when they get a letter from the ASA and many feel threatened and intimidated, with some being concerned that they may be sent to jail if they don't comply. It's not surprising that some practitioners feel they have no option but to shut down their practice."

The trouble began with an announcement that from March 2011 the CAP Code would apply to: "Advertisements and other marketing communications by or from companies, organisations or sole traders on their own websites, or in other non-paid-for space online under their control, that are directly connected with the supply or transfer of goods, services, opportunities and gifts, or which consist of direct solicitations of donations as part of their own fund-raising activities."

What this means is that the ASA regards your website as one big advertisement. The ASA has famously stated that CAM practitioners are subject to the same rules as companies selling roofing and guttering. Unfortunately, the ASA is unable and unwilling to treat complementary and alternative medicine with any subtlety, and it has brushed off concerns raised by both the Alliance for Natural Health International (ANH-Intl) and the CMA over its scientific competence to adjudicate complaints against CAM advertisers.

Making claims
Many claims CAM practitioners make, assert ANH-Intl and the CMA, are the result of decades of clinical experience, and are not necessarily limited to what can be found in the peer-reviewed literature, which tends to be both very limited and reductionist. However, the ASA remains adamant that any claims CAM practitioners make must be backed by at least one double-blind, placebo-controlled trial. It also seems to believe that the majority of health conditions should only be treated by medical doctors.

What this means that you are basically being blocked from telling the public what conditions your therapy can treat – and you certainly cannot publicise any successes you may have had with any particular named medical condition.

The CMA and ANH-Intl both believe that the future practice of CAM will be increasingly eroded if the ASA continues with its current heavy-handed policy.

Blocking websites and search engines
Early in 2012, the ASA announced at a meeting at the House of Commons reported in CAM magazine by Sophie Middleton, Campaign Administrator for Alliance for Natural Health Europe, that it had put in place agreements with Google to secure the

removal of paid advertisements for "non-compliers". They can also interfere with searches and put up adverts of their own to indicate where an individual, organisation or advert has been found to be guilty of non-compliant advertising.

No guidance
It has proved impossible to get any general guidelines from the ASA about precisely what CAM practitioners can or cannot say on websites – and in other practice materials. What we can say is that virtually anything you publish, even if you are trying to educate and inform, will be viewed as sales and marketing materials – and thus subject to the CAP Code.

We can infer from past rulings the kinds of things that really set them off. For example, cancer. On cancer the ASA acts as a censorship arm for orthodox medicine. We do not want to see people making claims that they can cure cancer. However, the ASA will also move against a bookstore advertising books detailing alternative philosophies and treatments for cancer. (It has done this with The Nutri Centre's announcements that it was stocking Prof Brian Peskin's "The Hidden Story of Cancer".) This is really going too far.

Some other ASA-isms: you will undoubtedly be told off if you describe yourself as a doctor, even if you have a doctorate – a PhD – and are entitled to. If you are a CAM practitioner the ASA will see this as you misleading the public into thinking you are a "real" doctor. Similarly, do not have a picture of yourself on your website wearing a white coat with a stethoscope draped round your neck, even if this is how you are used to dressing in clinic. Do not describe yourself as a "physician", either, even if you have the degree and title that comes with a training in Ayurvedic medicine.

Your clients don't know what they're saying
All the rules apply to testimonials, too. Here's an ASA ruling on a reflexology website:

"While we noted the testimonials may have been genuine opinions from clients, we noted we had not seen objective evidence that reflexology was able to have the benefits those clients claimed it could, such as treating depression or anxiety. We therefore concluded that the efficacy claims in the testimonials had not been substantiated.

"The claims breached CAP Code (Edition 12) rules 3.1 (Misleading advertising), 3.7 (Substantiation), 3.47 (Testimonials), 12.1, 12.2 and 12.6 (Medicines, medical devices, health-related products and beauty products)."

In other words, even if you have clients reporting improvements, the ASA will regard them as lying unless there is also "objective evidence" - they mean at least one double-blind placebo-controlled trial – to support what they say!

Do not use a list of medical conditions that you believe your therapy can help. It doesn't matter whether you have documented case histories. You will need evidence from double-blind placebo-controlled trials for each condition. And if they challenge you, they will expect you to send them copies of ALL the relevant studies, not just a list of references. They will pick you up on anything listed under "Main conditions treated" or "What conditions can we help you with?" They will be particularly hot on any conditions that, according to the ASA, "require" treatment from a medical doctor, even if clients are coming to see you precisely because that kind of treatment has already failed. Besides cancer, some of their other "red flag" conditions include asthma, high blood pressure, dizziness, bronchitis, menstrual disorders, menopause, impotence, infertility, prostate problems and depression.

Sad but true. There is no real way round this with careful wording. The ASA has, for instance, upheld complaints against a cranio-sacral therapy (CST) website whose owners went out of their way to state that its contents were based on the experiences of CST practitioners and clients rather than on scientific research, and that the references to specific conditions were not intended to imply or guarantee a cure for those, or other, conditions.

That didn't impress the ASA, who decided "consumers would understand the references to working with and helping specific named conditions, and more generally with, for example, situations, symptoms, traumas and injuries, to be factual statements relating to the experiences of CST practitioners and clients. We considered that consumers, including those who were familiar with complementary health approaches, would therefore understand those factual statements to be objective claims which were capable of substantiation. We considered that claims relating to experiences were akin to testimonials, and noted that CAP Code rule 3.47 required that claims which appeared in testimonials that were likely to be interpreted as factual must not mislead or be likely to mislead the consumer; we considered such claims must therefore be substantiated."

It then said: "We noted the statements in the ad to the effect that CST did not provide any guaranteed cures, and that the information provided in the ad should not be taken to mean that it could. However, we considered that such statements implied that whilst a cure for a condition was not guaranteed, it was possible that a condition could be cured by CST and, moreover, implied that conditions could be, at the least, alleviated by CST". Catch 22 anyone?

Tip 8 - Use colour to attract more clients

The Internet is a visual and psychological medium. Just as words can influence a client's response to your website, so can colour. The background colour of your website, the colour of your header, the colour of your text, headlines and sub-headlines etc can all have a psychological impact on your visitors. Here are common colours and what type of emotion they invoke in people:

RED is associated with love, passion, danger, warning, excitement, food, impulse, action, adventure.

BLUE is associated with trustworthiness, success, seriousness, calmness, power, professionalism.

GREEN is associated with money, nature, animals, health, healing, life, harmony.

ORANGE is associated with comfort, creativity, celebration, fun, youth, affordability.

PURPLE is associated with royalty, justice, ambiguity, uncertainty, luxury, fantasy, dreams.

WHITE is associated with innocence, purity, cleanliness, simplicity.

YELLOW is associated with curiosity, playfulness, cheerfulness, amusement.

PINK is associated with softness, sweetness, innocence, youthfulness, tenderness.

BROWN is associated with earth, nature, tribal, primitive, simplicity.

GREY is associated with neutrality, indifference, a sense of reserve.

BLACK is associated with seriousness, darkness, mystery, secrecy.

Blues and white backgrounds work best for business sites. Use red text when you are trying to catch someone's attention: "CALL US NOW!"

A white background focuses people's attention on the subject of the site. For example, look at the home page of Google. Acres of white! The focus of the page is the search box. Google spent millions on perfecting the best response colours.

As far as using colours in text, black text on white backgrounds may seem dull, but actually it is the most readable. White text reversed out of a black background, or yellow text on a white background...avoid these supposedly high-impact or "creative" touches; they are virtually unreadable and will have people straining to read them – and making a quick exit from your site.

Some of the most successful practitioners in the world all seem to use the same colours on their websites: blue, purple, green, all appear somewhere.

Tip 9 - Link to sites you like

Google, like most of the other leading search engines, is fully automated. It sends out software known as "spiders" or "bots" that crawl round the web looking for sites to add to the index. But here's a tip from The Google itself: "Googlebot crawls the web by following links from one page to another, so if your site isn't well linked, it may be hard for us to discover it".

Adding links to other sites also has another advantage – if you ask nicely they may add a reciprocal link to your site. This all helps increase the number of visitors you'll get, and can do wonders for your visibility. Don't just list websites you like, also include links to your favourite bloggers.

Tip 10 - Get your site up NOW

Every time Mark does a training or practitioner coaching session, there's one thing that always sets his alarm bells ringing. (It's not pretty!) That's when a student or client confidently announces that their website will be up and running in four weeks max (or less), because they have "a friend who does websites".

It very rarely works out. They're usually doing your website as a favour, in their spare time and/or at a reduced cost. What's promised in weeks, generally takes months.

If you go this route and you are lucky, you may have a half-finished website in two to three months. It's been known to take longer.

So: avoid using friends as website designers. Your website will be up and running much quicker if you deal with an independent designer. There you'll get the high level of commitment you need to get your site up and running as quickly as possible, normally in around four weeks. Time is of the essence when trying to get your website up the Google rankings.

Mark's Modelling Tip

Don't put off starting your website because you are waiting to finish your course. Once your website is completed it can take many weeks, maybe even months, before it stands a chance of getting on the front page of a Google search result. Get your website up as soon as possible.

Reaching the Top Rankings

Let's consolidate our knowledge and look at the key factors that will get your website to the top of Google:

- 95% of SEO happens through the home page
- website colours to attract visitors
- powerful website words
- Key Words mentioned twice
- Key Words focused on services products and location
- number of site visitors
- how long site has been up
- use of guarantees
- achieving a high quality score
- understanding and use of Google Analytics
- regular site reviews
- link to other sites

Once your site is finished and fully optimised you must then prepare for the long wait to get your site into the top five on page one of every relevant search result. This will be what is known as an organic listing, which simply means there's been no payment involved (as with use of Google AdWords, which we cover next).

Your success now depends on two things

1. How many people click on your website
2. The time it takes for Google to index your site and begin to score it.

Mark's Modelling Tip

After your site is launched you need to encourage as many people to click on it as possible. This will help your Google ranking.

Send a message to all your Facebook friends, Tweet about its launch, inform your LinkedIn network and email everybody else you know! Tell them you've launched a new website and ask them to go and have a good look around the site and give you feedback.

• Proactive advertising campaigns

Don't waste thousands of pounds advertising in places where you don't see any return on your investment.

Some practitioners take out ads in many different magazines, in the local press, in directories and on many specialist websites that promise a great response. Take a minute and think about your ideal client and where and when they decide they need someone just like you. When they make the decision, where are they going to look for you? Are they going to scan the local paper or freebie magazine, or look in the health magazine they picked up at their local gym?

As we now know that almost 100% of Internet users search for local businesses online, and 63% of people use the Internet FIRST when looking for a local service, the odds are pretty high that they are going to go online to find a practitioner.

Print advertising does work, but it needs to be consistent. And that can get expensive when you are first starting out. Think how much it would cost you to be in a magazine for 52 weeks of the year just to make sure you're there to be seen when the client might need you.

You'll save money and get quicker results for your start-up practice when you have a permanent presence in the place where the client is most likely to look for you, at any time of the day or night: online. You have to be there. The single most successful, cost-effective way to advertise is via Google AdWords.

What are Google AdWords?

Google AdWords are the advertisements with little blue words that you'll often see in the right-hand column of the page when you do a search on Google, or highlighted at the very top and/or bottom of the page in a different colour.

They are a fantastic way to reach your target market. You have the ability to run multiple ads targeted with one or more search key words, while Google's step-by-step demos walk you through the process of creating a successful ad campaign. You can have an AdWords campaign up and running in minutes and you can let it run for as long (or as short) as you want.

If you pay for (or "sponsor" in Googlespeak) the words "complementary medicine" and "Birmingham", for example, then your ad – which is a direct link to your website – will appear on the first page of results when anyone types "complementary medicine Birmingham" into Google.

The great thing about AdWords is that they are based on a Pay per Click system– so you only pay when someone clicks on your ad.

In summary:

- you are in complete control of how much you spend
- you can start and stop a campaign at any time
- you can set a maximum daily spend
- you choose the words you want to sponsor
- you design your own Google advert
- you can run as many ads as you want at any one time
- you only pay when someone visits your website
- you get statistical support to help you improve your campaign
- you can choose the best time of day for your ads to appear

As a bonus, a Google AdWords campaign will also help push your website up the Google organic listing as it generates more visitors to your site.

How much should you spend?

Set your advertising budget when you are forecasting your income and costs. Aim to spend a minimum of 20% of your gross turnover on advertising and when you are starting up spend this entire amount on monthly proactive advertising through Google AdWords.

So if you are a practitioner turning over £15,000 a year, then spending £3,000 a year on advertising would be about right - as a minimum. Assuming an average turnover for most full-time professional practitioners is £25,000 a year, a starting point for setting a Google budget would be a minimum of £5,000. We're saying "minimum" here, as it's common not to spend enough on advertising and to go at it somewhat half-heartedly. Your business will suffer as a result.

Here's an example of how it all works. Pretend you are a newly-qualified nutritional therapist who has just set up your first practice in Hitchin, Hertfordshire. You have a new website; you anticipate it will take several months for it to achieve a prominent position on Google. But you need clients immediately and can't wait. You decide to set up a Google AdWords campaign to get some clients and start earning a salary as a priority

Step 1   You go to www.google.co.uk/AdWords and follow the steps to set up your first campaign.

Step 2   You may choose to call 0800 169 0705 for step by step advice.

Step 3   You decide on the keywords you want to sponsor; these cover what you're offering potential clients, where you are, and also specifically targeted locations.

Step 4   Your keywords may include

- Nutritional Advice Hitchin
- Nutritional Advice Hertfordshire
- Nutritional Therapist Hitchin Hertfordshire
- Nutritional Consultations Hitchin
- Nutrition for Weight Loss Hitchin
- Nutrition for Stress Hertfordshire

Step 5   You log your chosen keywords onto your campaign. It's common to have several hundred keywords all costing different amounts per click Remember, you don't pay anything unless someone clicks on your website. To give you an idea of current costs per click, Nutritional Therapist Hitchin costs 15p.

Step 6 Decide how much more than the first page suggested price per click you want to pay and confirm your price per click. Remember, you must be in the top 5 of Google to be found continuously. Aim at bidding 15% over the suggested Google first page price to make sure you get a good placement. (Ads from people who bid more will appear above yours.)

Step 7 Set a daily budget and time span. For example, a £5 per day budget would cost you about £120 a month. For that sum several hundred potential clients may visit your website and not only push up your organic Google ranking, but more importantly some will become clients. Research across a variety of different therapies shows that you can expect on average to obtain 1 new client from every 4 enquiries. Of course, your results may vary: you never know for sure. Similarly, you can expect 4 enquiries from every 20-30 clicks onto your website. You will see how easy it is to work out from this how many clients your £120 should provide you with. All of these numbers will vary from therapy to therapy and according to how effective your website is. Also, the better you become at dealing with your enquiries the more clients you will get.

Step 8 Review your progress every week using Google Analytics and make the appropriate changes to keep enhancing your results. You may want to trial different key words to see which words work best for you. You may wish to review your budget depending on your results. A good tip is to put aside a sum of money, say £25, and set a limit of £5 per day - that will give you five days of prime advertising. A good time to advertise is late afternoons, as people spend more time online in the evenings. Also the big AdWords spenders will have exhausted their budgets by that late in the day, giving the likes of us a chance to reach the top.

• Putting social media to work for you

Social Media represents a shift in how people discover, read and share news and information and communicate with each other.

One Tweet from a famous sportsman can now reach millions of fans in seconds. The rap star Eminem, allegedly has the most Facebook fans of any celebrity: he has more than 56 million followers! LinkedIn had 4,500 members in its network for professionals at the end of its first month in operation in 2003; by mid-2012 it had more than 175 million in more than 200 countries and territories.

Then there are blogs. By the end of 2011, NM Incite, a Nielsen/McKinsey company, tracked more than 181 million blogs around the world, up from 36 million only five years earlier in 2006. The Huffington Post grew out of a blog started by Arianna Huffington in 2005. It is now a fully-fledged "Internet newspaper" that has even won a Pulitzer Prize; it is the most widely-read blog in the world, attracting a monthly audience of around 54 million unique visitors.

This is a real revolution. It is changing the way we contact, influence, attract and ultimately do business with our clients. We practitioners need to acknowledge the power of social media and its reach and influence. We need to become as comfortable with using social media as we are with our computers. Most successful practitioners use (at least) Facebook, Twitter and LinkedIn, the three main social media tools, and you will notice the famous logos somewhere on the home page of their websites.

We're going to hand over to Social Media Expert Penny Homer to explain the essentials. But first a word about webinars and podcasts.

Again, these are so new to some of us that they hurt. But they are simple and easy strategies you can use to reach more people, faster and more cost-effectively than ever before.

Webinars

Short for Web-based Seminar. Many practitioners have caught on to this and are making short educational or informative videos and placing them on their websites or linking to their own dedicated channel on YouTube. This is a great way to raise your profile, reaches a worldwide audience and grabs the attention of tv-trained clients who would rather watch a movie than read.

Eventually you can take this to the next level and run a one-hour (or less) evening lecture or seminar on a subject you are expert in and have your clients join you live on the Net. They can phone, email or text you questions while you are online.

Podcasts

Apple describes a podcast (from "broadcast" and "iPod"), as being like a tv or radio show – with episodes you can download and play. iTunes, the Apple site, has more than 100,000 podcasts – all free. Follow their lead and have clients and visitors to your site subscribe to your podcasts which will download more or less automatically to their computers as soon as you release your latest "episode".

You'll see a lot of natural health sites producing audio podcasts instead of or as well as blogs and news reports. It's easier to just record an interview with someone, or yourself answering questions, and stick it on your website, than it is to write the thing out. So again, it's a quick, easy and effective way of reaching people.

Now over to Penny's "How to Win with Social Media".

How to Win with Social Media

Penny Homer

The expansion of social media has created opportunities for practitioners to reach out to potential clients, create new professional networks and build on relationships with existing clients (should they wish to be public).

This guide gives you some tips on how to build your social media profile and use it to grow your business, as well as manage the associated risks.

What is social media?
Social Media is an umbrella term for a number of online or mobile platforms that enable individuals and organisations to communicate and network with each other.

This includes networks and blogging sites such as Facebook, Twitter, YouTube, Wordpress, Tumblr, Pinterest, LinkedIn, Google+ and Wikipedia, although it should be noted that this list is not exhaustive and new platforms are constantly being developed.

Why do social media?
This is possibly the most important question to ask before using social media for business (or even at all) – why are you doing it?

You wouldn't work with a client without setting goals and developing ways to reach them, so why would you make this mistake with social media?

Before starting to build any profile on social media, you should consider what it is you hope to gain as a result.

Set targets, whether it be increased followers, referrals through social media, other professional connections made, how much your content is shared - these will vary from practitioner to practitioner.

There are, however, some basics that can help you raise your profile, bring in new clients and grow your business.

Pick your platforms wisely

The sheer number of social media platforms out there is overwhelming, and it's growing every day. So which ones should you use?

Blogs - Wordpress, Blogspot etc

This is your number 1 tool for growing your business through social media.

Why? One word - content.

Use your blog to write about aspects of your business - trends within your field, your opinion on news stories that relate to your field, tips for success, and even case studies, if you have clients who are willing to share their stories (they can do so either publicly or remain anonymous).

Link it to a contact detail, or your homepage, and you have a call to action.

You can then share this using every other social media platform, and use it to influence your targeted communities. For instance, placing on Twitter or Facebook a link to a blogpost can massively increase the amount of times it is viewed, and the chances for people to click through to your website or email.

LinkedIn

LinkedIn is, in simplest terms, the biggest networking event you can attend, and it's 24 hours. Working on the degrees of separation principle, you connect with your existing business network. You can then see who they are connected to - it could be another practitioner looking for someone with your skills to team up with - and expand your network from there.

The groups function also allows you to find people from your own sector - for instance groups interested in herbal medicine, bodywork, nutrition or NLP - where individuals gather to share referrals and good practice. So not only does this increase your network and potential referrals, but it also allows you to stay up to date with the latest trends in your field.

If your clients are happy to be public, they can recommend your services on LinkedIn. This is an extraordinarily powerful tool - potential clients are able to see that your current clients are very happy with the service you provide. You can use those recommendations over and over again - remember you can link to LinkedIn from other platforms (Facebook, Twitter et al).

You can advertise on LinkedIn, however for this industry a huge return would be unlikely. It's better to use this to build a network on your own.

Facebook
Facebook is the tool for building your business through your existing clients.

Creating a page for your business on Facebook gives another chance to share content.

Invite your clients to like your page, and they can then share that content with their friends (this is where the tips for success blogs work so well). You can also invite discussion with your page's fans by posing questions relating to an element of your practice.

These actions increase your fans and demonstrate to them (whether they be existing clients or potential new ones) that you know your field. From this grows the chance of increased referrals and new business.

Twitter
Possibly the most powerful tool for sharing information and building new communities there is right now.

This network enables you to post short updates (up to 140 characters) and follow the updates of anyone you want. There are also hashtags, which enable users to find people tweeting about a topic, event or news story that interests them. The retweet function also provides a way for people to quickly share content they like - so again, get a good blogpost up there and it could be seen by thousands of people you never would've reached before.

People often ask about how to get more followers. There are ways to do that, but that also misses the point of Twitter. You can have 10,000 followers, but they might not result in a single referral. What you want is a solid base of followers who are listening to what you have to say, and want to share it with their followers.

Here are some tips for doing that:

1. Don't go on a 'following' spree
Many users see an account that is following lots of people but has few followers as potential spam, especially if the account is a corporate one. Use the search function to find people you find interesting, be they within your field, local community, friends or personal interests.

2. Talk to people, not at them
Twitter users like to see that an account engages in conversation with other users, rather than just broadcasting. When looking at a user's profile, Twitter initially shows the 3 most recent tweets from that profile. If it's all broadcast tweets with links,

people are likely to disregard that account, unless it is a large organisation like a newspaper. So do make an effort to engage with people.

3. Listen
Twitter is fantastic as a way of finding out things - a networking event in your area you didn't know about, a new idea in your field - so don't forget to listen as well as talk.

4. Have fun
Users like to see a sense of humour. It makes you appear more rounded as an individual, rather than just being "all business". This builds trust among your followers.

5. Be polite.
Again, an obvious one, but with the rise of Internet trolling it's clear that many people have failed to take note of this simple rule.

When expressing opinions, don't get aggressive or swear, and avoid singling particular people out for criticism. Since your target client base (and thus followers) is likely to have wide ranging views on politics and/or religion, it is best to steer clear of talking about these subjects in partisan terms.

Be careful as well in responding to criticism. It's never worth getting into a public slanging match.

6. Don't spam
This should be obvious, but you'd be surprised at how many people go around asking for retweets, referrals or business from people they've never interacted with before. One of the main points of Twitter is relationship building - do that first before you start asking for stuff. After all, would you go up to someone you'd never met at a networking meeting and immediately ask them for a referral? Of course not, so steer clear of it on Twitter. The Follow Friday idea, where you

recommend followers, also tends to be treated with suspicion and even annoyance. If you're going to do it, list each recommendation individually and give a good reason why people should follow them.

With all the excitement about social media, it's easy to forget that there are risks attached. Managing these risks can all be summed up in one sentence – "Think before you post".

Social networks are by their nature open. Anything that you post remains on the Internet indefinitely, and can be shared very easily with anyone. Even if your personal Facebook account, for example, has the privacy settings turned up to the max, all it takes is for someone to press "print screen" and they can email a status to anyone they like. While this has good potential for sharing, make sure you're not sharing something you shouldn't.

So don't post anything that would violate client confidentiality. Of course this will be obvious to all of you, but it is surprising how much information people give away without meaning to. Similarly, be aware of how much you're giving away about yourself. As a rule, it's best not to post pictures that can make it easy to locate your house and/or other valuables. If you're telling social media about where you are and who you are with – you are potentially also telling criminals that there's no one at your house.

Information obtained through social media can be used to impersonate someone's identity, so be careful about giving away too much - you could give away your date of birth, address and mother's maiden name over various networks over the course of time without even realising it!

Be careful of any private messages, especially on Twitter, telling you for example that someone is saying something bad about you, and inviting you to click on a link. If the message looks a little odd, don't click the link as this is likely to be an attempt to hack your account.

If you follow these simple ideas, you'll be well on your way to building a good social media presence. Combine this with setting CSMART targets and your social media presence will be a key tool for growing your business.

Penny Homer, Social Media coordinator and Sales Operations Manager, Edition Peters Group : homerpenny@ gmail.com

---

• Data marketing - your newsletter

What can a newsletter do for you? Let's hear from e-newsletter expert Michael Katz, founder and Chief Penguin at Blue Penguin Development, and the man industry leaders in the email marketing field turn to for advice.

"A quality E-Newsletter attracts people to you and makes everything about your business run more smoothly" he says. Specifically, he says:

- It brings you new, pre-qualified prospects
- It turns old prospects into clients
- It generates more business with your existing clients
- It positions you as an industry expert
- It gets you exposure in search engines
- It gives you a place to develop and refine new ideas and techniques
- It provides an opportunity for shaping and articulating your vision
  (Sourced from the home of Michael's excellent e-newsletter course: www.enewslettersystem.com)

Your newsletter is the reason we've been emphasising the need to set up your website to encourage people to give you their email addresses. In addition, get neurotic about collecting email addresses and permissions. Your intake questionnaire undoubtedly has a space for clients to fill in their email address; it should also ask for their permission for you to send them your weekly newsletter. Collect email addresses and permissions from every enquiry, every conversation.

Sending out a regular newsletter keeps you in the minds of your clients and potential client. They may have never contacted you, but they liked the look of your site and the information you provided...now they're reading your newsletter. You're building a solid relationship and you haven't even met or spoken to them yet.

So begins a process of data marketing which will prove critical to your business over the first 12 months of trading. You are creating what Mark calls "relationships for tomorrow". When they or someone they know needs a professional CAM practitioner who will they think of? You. Who will they talk about when they share their newly-discovered health tips? You. So you are creating a base of referrals as well.

Most CAM practitioners don't have a newsletter. They think it's too complicated, time consuming and difficult to set up. And anyway, what would they write about? What they're really saying is that they don't understand it, and if don't understand something it will frighten you. So let's show you how easy this all is.

Mark's Modelling Tip

Make it a non-negotiable minimum standard that you are going to collect an email address from everyone that you come into business contact with. These will include

- visitors to your website
- new clients
- client enquiries

- business partners
- other therapists and practitioners
- influential industry contacts

How to set up your newsletter

Setting up your first newsletter is very straightforward. Really. Most website hosting companies have an add-on facility that will expand your basic website email so that it can manage a newsletter database of around 500 names or more. This will probably work for you for your first 6-12 months in practice.

Your website or blog may be built with the free web software WordPress; if it is, you can find free "plug-ins" that automate the whole process of opting-in, getting permission and managing your newsletter database – and provides an automated opt-out/cancel subscription service as well.

As your database grows, we recommend using a specialist management system. It sounds expensive, but to run a newsletter for up to 5000 recipients, taking advantage of full visuals, links, and media facilities only costs from around £10 per month. For this you get everything you need, from templates to design, as well as some great advice.

(Our favourite company for this is Constant Contact ®: www.constantcontact.com, 0800 234 9315.)

How often should you send out your newsletter?

Shoot for once a week. Fortnightly at a minimum.

When should you send it out?

The same day every week to create consistency and continuity. When you have some special news to announce, perhaps dates for a new course or a new product, send out ad hoc in addition to your weekly newsletter. That way you won't dilute your original message.

What should I write about?

Ah, the final sticking point!

Put yourself solidly in your ideal client's shoes. What is going to be of most benefit to them? So: everything and anything you think will interest your potential client. Has there been a massive new story in the Daily Mail about a health issue, or a scare story about vitamins – if so, what's your take on it?

If you've found online good news stories about natural health, share the links with a brief comment explaining why they will find the story worth reading. If possible, tie this back to the work you do (without making claims).

Give them free health tips, recipes, info about good foods, tips about where to fund good quality food. Then there is the news from your practice – no, your new laser printer is not news; special money-off promotions, open days/evenings, discounted sessions, new protocols – that's news.

Chief Penguin Michael Katz, consultant to Constant Contact, says there are 4 Secrets to an effective newsletter. His guidelines are:

1. **Make it Useful**.
   People are barraged with emails, he says. You are constantly fighting their urge to hit the delete button. So, make sure that EVERY e-newsletter you send includes one highly useful bit of information. Michael talks about working to give them "some kind of actionable 'aha' with every issue".
2. **Make it Interesting**.
   Michael's take on this is that just because you want to be businesslike and professional doesn't mean you have to be serious and, well, downright boring. Keep it light, write to them as if you were talking to them and yes, it's OK to be funny and include personal anecdotes now and then.

3. **Make it Simple**.
   Keep it short and sweet. Not too much detail. No references. "An effective newsletter isn't a doctoral thesis; it's not even a case study. It's what I like to call, 'a nugget'", he says. "One insight or tip or concept that your readers can take in, understand, and hopefully remember long enough to put into practice."
4. **Make it Authentic**.
   Have your newsletter reflect your personality and the ethos of your practice. Yes, it should be different from everyone else's, because you are.

What happens when someone no longer wants your newsletter?

Make it easy for people to unsubscribe and be diligent about keeping on top of requests to be removed from your list. You should have an unsubscribe link on every newsletter you send out. This can be an automated link, if you have the technology, or a direct link to your own email. Keep checking that you have permission to include them.

If you don't have permission you are guilty of sending out spam. Industry leader Constant Contact® offers this warning about making absolutely sure you have permission:

"Once your email newsletters are marked as Spam, more Internet Service Providers (ISPs) will automatically put you in other Spam Mailboxes. And that's a small business nightmare. Permission-based email marketing is the answer, but your company still needs to keep readers happy (aka not annoyed)." You can download Constant Contact's guide with the ten best ways to improve your email marketing success rate here: http://img.constantcontact.com/docs/pdf/learn-how-to-get-and-keep-email-permission-constant-contact.pdf .

"Tips include:

- Beware of offers to purchase lists. "Permission is not transferable. Today, subscribers want to receive email from those companies they have subscribed to, not an unknown third party."
- Remind recipients why they are receiving your email newsletters
- Give your subscribers choices – some may just be interested in your nutrition services, others in hearing more about bodywork or coaching
- State your privacy policy clearly
- Invite your customers to take an online survey or poll to give feedback about your newsletter – it shows you are interested in their opinions
- Provide the most valuable info to each customer"

How many subscribers do you need?

Aim for 50 in the first 3 months and 100 by month 6. It's a reasonable, achievable goal to have 250 names on your newsletter data base by the end of your first year. By the end of year 3 you will probably be up to 1000. Remember you will get a handful of un-subscribers, so challenge yourself to replace them every month.

Word of mouth isn't random and it isn't luck

A final word about the importance of your newsletter from Michael Katz:

- As a professional service provider, you know that word of mouth is the primary (and best) way to get new clients.
- The prospects who come to you through referrals and recommendations are much more likely to become clients. In fact, the whole process of meeting

them, talking with them and ultimately starting work together is much easier and much more enjoyable than with a stranger.

- But you probably think of word of mouth as a fortunate, but random accident (I know that I used to). It isn't. With a systematic approach to staying in front of everybody you know (ie with a high quality e-newsletter), you'll generate word of mouth consistently and efficiently.

(Michael Katz: www.enewslettersystem.com)

Chapter 6: Essential Practitioner NLP skills

To run a successful clinic, you need a wide range of skills. You have to know how to run a business and you simply must have strong interpersonal and communication skills for dealing with clients.

When it comes down to it a lot of the essential skills are the same in dealing with a business as with clients. We can summarise them so:

Business skills

- Business knowledge & acumen
- Business focus & discipline
- Business vision & mission
- Business philosophy
- Ability to action plan
- Decision making
- Negotiating skills
- Motivation
- Time management
- Confidence
- Self-belief

Client facing skills

- Inspiration
- Motivation
- Leadership
- Strong interpersonal skills
- Listening
- Professionalism & credibility

- Integrity
- Rapport building skills
- Organisation
- Time management
- Knowledge of subject
- Confidence
- Self-belief

We're going to focus on the client facing skills. This skill-set is vital to your success – that's obvious. Just by looking at that list you can see how essential they are in practice. Yet amazingly, it's possible to go through an entire CAM certificate, diploma or degree course and never have them mentioned.

We're going to use NLP – introduced briefly in chapter 2 - as the core strategy when establishing and developing Key Practitioner Skills. That's not only because both of us are trained in NLP and use it every day, but also because NLP is famously renowned for giving practitioners a wide range of relationship-building skills, enabling them to confidently deal with clients. It's also relatively easy to grasp.

The first CAM degree course to embrace a formal training in NLP as part of its curriculum was the Centre for Nutrition Education and Lifestyle Management. Kate Neil, CAM's foremost nutritional therapy educator, recalls why she took the leap:

"There are a few select types of practitioners, like nutritional therapists and personal trainers, where so much of the outcome for the client is going to depend on the client's ability to change and to sustain change.

"General generic counselling – which is basically a practitioner being nice to a person - doesn't necessarily help. When a client leaves a nutritional therapist's room they're thinking 'How am I going to put that into action, how will this affect my relationships with children, family, friends, people at work...'

Even if someone lives alone, they are probably still going to work and having other people questioning their food choices, not to mention that they are potentially still liking and craving the food they're already eating – so it's a huge area of difficulty in being able to make changes and sustain a programme."I felt that incorporating a coaching model would give nutritional therapists more skills in their toolbox to help people work through their attitudes, limiting beliefs and so on and help create goals. We also want practitioners to be able to get into other people's maps of the world, rather than to keep banging on about how you see things, and when the client comes back they're still doing what they were doing - or they don't come back at all.

"That's why back in 2003 I thought I would really like to include coaching skills and NLP was accessible to us, whereas to try to include something like CBT (cognitive behavioural therapy) would involve a much more prolonged programme of study. I felt that NLP was coherent, cohesive – you could teach quality skills in the context of a 17-day NLP practitioner course and students could grasp something tangible. They really see it making a difference in their success as practitioners."

Kate reports that nutritional therapists using NLP consultation skills see that it makes a change in three key areas:

* Clients find it easier to make and sustain change
* Compliance is improved: clients are more likely to do what the practitioner has recommend
* Clients come back!

We asked Kate how a nutritional therapy consultation might go when the practitioner is trained in NLP. It seems a major difference is that before starting in on a traditional history-taking, the client is encouraged to start thinking about what they really want to achieve – about change, and what might help or hinder it.

"What we're aiming for when they take a full nutritional therapy consultation" Kate says, "is to start with proper NLP-type questioning about goal-setting. For example, asking questions to find out what advantages the client sees in a change, and what advantages are there for them staying as they are. We ask questions like, "What things do you see would hold you back from that?" "Where would you like to be in 6 months, or 3 months?" That way you can start to get a frame around it even before you start asking the specific nutritional therapy questions."

At the end of the history-taking when the client has talked about their specific health problems, the practitioner revisits the client's goals and feelings about change and sees if they are still the same. A standard NLP reality check. "When you are making your recommendations you can keep referring to their goals and where they are at, and keep reinforcing it." NLP emphasises the importance of joining the client in their map of the world, not in forcing on them the practitioner's view of how things operate. That demands that the practitioner uses the client's language – their exact words and phrases they use to describe their condition – not translating it into therapeutic jargon. That continues right through to the end of the consultation, when the therapist is writing up recommendations. As we'll explain, this use of language helps you, as a practitioner, really step into the client's reality and see what and how they are dealing with things. It is also very encouraging for the client, who may even remark to you that it's the first time that a health practitioner has ever really listened to them.

As Kate concludes, NLP offers "very powerful, useful and accessible tools."

(Kate Neil, MSc (Nutritional Medicine), mBANT, NTCC, CNHC, is the managing director of the Centre for Nutrition Education and Lifestyle Management (CNELM), a former director of the Institute of Optimum Nutrition and was part of the team that developed the first degree course in nutritional therapy at the University of Westminster, where she supervised clinical training. CNELM was the first nutrition degree course programme to adopt a coaching model and to include NLP. CNELM is the only private centre in the UK delivering a nutritional therapy undergraduate degree course (BSc Hons) that is fully validated by a university (the University of Middlesex): www.cnelm.co.uk)

The client cycle

Before we dive in to the essential NLP skills, let's look at the typical behaviour of a client looking for a CAM practitioner.

1. Client wants a practitioner
2. Client researches and investigates suitable practitioners
3. Client finds several that seem suitable
4. Client emails all suitable practitioners
5. Client awaits response
6. Client checks again practitioner websites, services, prices and policy statements
7. Client exchanges information with practitioner
8. Client chooses most suitable practitioner

If we study this booking cycle, it's clear that it's only when the client reaches step 4 that the practitioner has a chance to be proactive and secure the client for her practice. There's a lot going on behind the scenes before you get that chance; your ability to quickly build a relationship and establish a trustworthy professional connection has to be spot on.

• The Art of Building Rapport

Mark has never forgotten his trainer Alistair Horscroft, Living Television's Life Guru at the time, telling me that if you can quickly build strong rapport with a client you are 95% of the way to achieving a successful session.

"He was so right", Mark says. "Rapport opened the locks of doors never opened before, enabled me to get inside the thoughts of clients who hadn't been able to express themselves for years, and helped me change people's lives in a single session after only spending an hour with me."

Remember, rapport = Client trust, buy-in, commitment, focus, confidence and belief. No rapport = a lack of client trust, speculation, worry, doubt, and disbelief, Establishing rapport is the unchallenged, number 1 skill that all practitioners not only have to master but master with real style and vigour. Get this right and it will make the difference between your success and failure with clients.

Our natural ability to relate to others

Some of us seem to flow through life getting on with everyone and are confident in our ability to naturally build rapport with other people. Others struggle, are shy and really find it difficult to strike up "small talk" conversations with people they don't know.

This is mainly down to self-confidence and self-belief. We've said it before: a lack of understanding naturally breeds fear. We are afraid of what we don't know and understand. You know by now that a huge component of NLP – and success – is modelling. The developers of NLP originally observed some of the world's most amazing psychotherapists in action; these people were superb at gaining rapport with even the most introverted, closed-down clients. Thanks to NLP modelling we know exactly what they did and how they did it, and that's what you can now easily learn. When you know and understand the "secrets" of rapport, you too will have confidence and self-belief that you can get along with anyone.

In a nutshell, rapport is the ability to join someone in their "reality" - or "map of the world" as Kate referred to it, and to make them feel comfortable. They will feel that you have a strong common bond and that you understand them. These are the things that put people at ease, make them more responsive to you and make them more likely to trust, like and befriend you. What stops this from being a manipulative sales technique is that rapport is a two-way street. You are effectively opening yourself up to another person and really feeling what it is like to experience the world as they do.

If you want to come at this in a more "out there" way, then think of this: it's true that people like people who are like themselves. The old cliché that "opposites attract' is actually just a misunderstanding of the depth and subtlety that rapport goes to. When "opposites attract" it usually means that the so-called opposites have in common the ability to be excited by the new and different, the sense of specialness and uniqueness of being "opposites". In fact when you really experience rapport in action, you will inevitably realise that (even in so-called "opposites"), we are all much more similar to each other than we are different. This is a very deep level of communication.

OK, back down to earth. Practical matters: how can you create rapport? There was a clue above. First and foremost by finding things you have in common. The most effective ways of doing this are by mirroring and matching - two concepts that originated in NLP.

• Mirroring and Matching

Mirroring is essentially copying and reflecting back your client's physical patterns of behavior, without causing offence and without being obvious. Matching is almost identical as a concept, but normally involves the person's map of the world, their language and beliefs, not just physical mannerisms. Here we'll use the word matching to include mirroring.

Matching subtly tells the other person that you are rather like them. It can make them feel totally at ease and fully responsive to what you have to say. Watch two close friends talking and you'll see matching in all its glory. Matching can be done in a great variety of ways:

Whole body matching

Adjust your body to approximate the other person's physical position and behavior - head, arms, legs, toes, hands, feet, fingers etc.

Gestures

Match the person's gestures - hand waving, crossing arms or legs, finger movements, head tilts etc.

Facial Expressions

Match movement of ears, eyebrows, eyelids, jaw position, nose twitches, mouth movements etc.

Breathing

One of the best – match pattern, rate, depth, location.

Vocal characteristics

Match word and sentence length, volume, tempo, accent (don't overdo this!), recurring words and phrases they use etc.

If you pay attention to what you do when you are talking to a loved one, you'll see how this is done in a way that builds rapport. However be warned you can get too self-aware. When you catch yourself raising your tea cup at exactly the same time of your spouse, all the time, it can get a bit much! If you go too over the top with this with someone you've just met, then consciously or unconsciously, they will come to the conclusion that you are mimicking them, and this can lead to trouble So do not practise on strangers in the pub.

In the clinic, if you get it wrong, you will instantly lose rapport. So take it easy. If you are ANY good at all at talking to people, then you will see you are probably doing some or all of this already. In which case notice the areas – tone and rhythm of speech, for instance – that you are not doing well, or at all, and practice them. Practise this in shops, family interactions and with friends. Push it until they notice, but start very subtly, just matching a few of their behaviors. When someone is in heightened emotional state they normally become more sensitive to mimickry, so be careful. You can of course get equally fired up with them or upset with them and keep rapport that way!

As an example from practice, Simon had a client who just would not look him in the eye when they were talking. She would look down at the floor – anywhere. With eye contact she would become very hesitant... "I was getting more stressed out with every session", he recalls. "I had convinced myself I just wasn't getting through to her, but she seemed to get something out of the sessions. Baffling." One day, just before the session started she took a phone call. She was transformed. She spoke quickly, articulately and at length, and was very animated. As soon as the call was over: back to "normal". Finally the penny dropped; in NLP terms, she was highly auditory. Her preferred way of processing information was to listen. If she looked at someone's face during a conversation she lost the plot.

There's a lesson about being willing and able to join someone in their map of the world. In this case, a map where meeting someone's eyes when they talk to you doesn't mean you are being polite, honest, open and communicative – it's just a distraction.

• Pacing and Leading

Once rapport is created we then use it to "pace and lead" the client in the direction that we believe is most beneficial to them. It is also a barometer that lets us know when rapport has been broken. We pace - continually match - the client and lead them to more resourceful, constructive and beneficial states, behaviours and beliefs etc.

A graphic physical example of this comes from Simon's running coaching sessions. He is often working with people who say they "can't run" or they "can't run fast". You start out where they are, maybe jogging alongside them very very slowly. If you match their gait, stride length, footfall, their breathing, there will come a point, inevitably, where the two of you are in synch. If the coach then starts to relax and run faster, the "I can't run" client will follow right along, even changing their style as they do so. That's how it works. You're looking for that moment of synching, what some bodyworkers describe as the "hook-up"; then your client will follow you into optimism, relaxation, wherever you want to go, as long as they feel it is in their best interests.

Just like the "slow" (and often injured) runners, your clients do have the resources they need for healing, but they have got so used to living with chronic fatigue or endless gut pain that they have completely lost sight of their "inner" healthy self. It's no use rubbing your hands together briskly and jovially and loudly announcing "We'll soon have you sprinting a mile" to your tired and pained clients: what a mismatch! Think about where they are and how you can meet them there.

• Presuppositions

NLP Practitioners adopt a certain set of assumptions, or "presuppositions", as they are commonly known. Mark always refers to these as Empowering Beliefs.

They are really a set of assumptions about how the world works that many NLP practitioners adopt, as assuming or pre-supposing that they are "true" seems to help achieve success and an easier, more fulfilling life. There are a number of different versions although the main integral presuppositions remain constant. Here we're focusing on Mark's favourite 13.

By implementing these empowering beliefs into your daily life and into the way you run your practice, you will see a significant change not only in the results you achieve in your business, but also desired changes in your personal life as well.

A good idea is to learn these one at a time; play with a few until you get the hang of them and then move on. One of our favourite books on NLP is "NLP in 21 Days" (Piatkus Books, 2000). In it, Harry Alder and Beryl Heather not only explain the basic practices of NLP, but introduce one presupposition a day for you to play with. It's a good introduction.

1. **The map is not the territory**

   Without doubt the most famous of all of the presuppositions. The context for this is that we all make a subjective "map" of the world that may bear no resemblance to the "real" word – aka external reality.

   It's this internal, subjective representation (the map) that we respond to, not external reality itself. In our endless search for meaning we consult our map to make sense of our feelings and experiences. This is "glass half full", "glass half empty" territory. Some people's map of the world is such that everything is a problem; to others, faced with the same "reality", life is full of opportunities. We're reminded of Arthur Smith and the other Grumpy Old Men in the tv series. Arthur's view was along the lines of "Every day you know you're going to go out of the house and something is going to annoy you".

   The great thing about this is that once we realise and accept that our map of the world is not actually "real" but just our perception of the way things are, then we realise that we can change the map whenever we want.

2. Respect all maps are different

We acknowledge and understand that everybody's map is different and we learn to respect that others don't see the world the same way we do.

3. Expand your map

By aiming to increase choice, you're choosing to expand your map of reality. Expand your map to one that gives you the widest and richest number of choices. The more choices you have, the freer you are and the more influence you have over yourself and others.

As Rudyard Kipling said, for example: "I always prefer to believe the best of everybody; it saves so much trouble".

The broader our perspectives now, the more choices we have – in the past, present and future...

4. We don't judge the behaviors of others

No one is wrong or broken. People function perfectly even if what they are doing is ruining their life. All behavior has a structure. When you understand the structure, you can change the behavior into something more desirable.

Doing the behavior is just an effect of the cause. Establish the cause and you can change the behavior

6. The meaning of your communication is in the response you get

Resistance in others indicates a lack of rapport, or that the other person doesn't get your meaning. We all resist when we don't understand. Your intended communication is not always what is perceived and this presupposition throws the responsibility for effective communication right back at you.

Which is more important: what you intend to communicate, or what you actually communicate?

Flexible communicators change what they're saying (and how they're saying it, as well as their body language) until their desired results are obtained.

7. We already have all the resources we need to get what we want

You already have it in you. Everything a person needs to effect a positive change is already in them. They may, however, not be consciously aware of it. Often people have resources that they haven't considered or that are only available in other contexts. They may be super-organised at work and completely chaotic in their personal life to the extent that relationships suffer.

By "resources" we mean the internal responses and external behaviors needed to get desired results. Our most basic resource is our ability to learn.

There are no unresourceful people, only unresourceful states of mind. As response-able people, we can run our own minds and therefore move towards getting the results that we want. The key to achieving this is through knowing how to change your state, as specific resources are accessed only through being in the appropriate state. States are the keys that either open or lock the door to the infinite reservoir of resources inside you.

8. There is no such thing as failure, there is only feedback

Every experience offers a lesson, one from which we can grow intellectually or in terms of emotional intelligence. Living is learning; even if you lose, you don't lose the learning

Every result gives you feedback, maybe information about how to do something differently next time. Feedback is helpful and sets direction. This kind of attitude toward "failure" produces results that allow you to improve. Results are the means by which you measure your progress and adjust your behavior in order to achieve your desired outcomes.

The epitome of this is Thomas Edison, the inventor of the light bulb, who allegedly "failed" more than 1,000 times to get a bulb to work. When challenged, he famously commented: "I have not failed, not once. I've discovered ten thousand ways that don't work." (Source: apocryphal, probably true, but the original quote has never been traced.)

9. There is a positive intention behind every behavior

Our actions are not random; we are always trying to achieve something good, although we may not be aware of what that is.

As practitioners this gives us a unique way of looking at people's problems. When it is clear that their current behavior is contributing to their health condition, we know to dig deeper to find out what is it that they are trying to achieve – often simply the avoidance of pain or the acquisition of pleasure – that is having unintended consequences, and we can the help them find a healthier way of getting that.

NLP separates the intention or purpose behind an action from the action itself. A person is not their behavior. When a person has a better choice of behavior that also achieves their positive intention, they will take it.

10 Individual flexibility = maximum control

In any field, the top people are those who have the most variety in their behavior. They have choices of behavior that their colleagues don't. Any time you limit your behavioral choices you give others the competitive edge. If in any situation you have a variety of ways that you can respond, you are more likely to get your outcome.

This is important to you as a practitioner. Do you have one protocol that you are going to use on everyone? One of the therapy greats NLP modelled was the psychiatrist Dr Milton Erikson, MD. He was flexibility personified. Dr Stephen Gilligan studied with Erickson and modeled him. ""Erickson worked... in locked wards of mental hospitals", says Gilligan. "One guy insisted he was Jesus Christ, despite the many efforts by staff to convince him otherwise. Erickson introduced himself to 'Jesus', let him know that there was a new ward being built on hospital grounds that needed some carpenters, and got 'Jesus' to work as a carpenter. His work led him to become involved with other folks, which eventually led him back into common reality." (http://www.stephengilligan.com/interviewA.html)

11 Modelling successful performance leads to excellence

Modelling is one of the key presuppositions of NLP. Why re-invent the wheel, with is attendant risk of "failure" (which we will now refer to as potentially many years of feedback!)? Make it one of your early practice non-negotiables: only model success.

No matter how you define success, many successful people have got to where they are through modelling the successful performance of others.

Find a model of excellence in a field that you're interested in. Identify the sequence of components (thoughts, beliefs, values and behaviors) that are necessary to achieve the desired result. Apply that model in a way that enables you to get the same kinds of results, and success is yours.

12 If you want results – keep taking action

Real learning is in the doing. Through application you will soon discover what works and what doesn't work. Keep doing the things that get you the results that you want. Remember, there is no failure, only feedback.

13 Wisdom model

In life it is very easy to focus on our achievements all the time; on reflection we may see that sometimes we beat ourselves up over whether we have achieved a specific outcome or not.

NLP teaches us to simply reframe that thinking to focus more on the process. What have we learned from the experience, whether we fully achieved our goal or not? And how can we improve our performance next time?

• Unlocking your potential

When you decide to do something for the first time it's natural to have some anxiety. "Will everything be all right, will I perform OK?" and so forth. When you start your own business it is exactly the same. It's common to experience a range of emotions, from fear to indecision, to uncertainty, self-doubt and so on.

Once you have read this book and embraced all of your new learnings, beliefs and strategies we GUARANTEE you will be experiencing a different set of emotions! Some nerves may remain, but generally you will feel much more excited, enthusiastic, motivated and - most importantly - in control. After all, you'll have something you didn't have before: a strategy, a plan and, if you have followed our advice all the way, you've found a successful therapist to model.

What we need to focus on now is making a mental shift to maximize our full potential. It's all very well having a plan, but how to we attain that mental state that will enable us to take action to achieve the results we need? How do we create and retain a successful practice?

There's an idea making the rounds that 1% of the population control 99% of the wealth. Can this be true? Why are some people so much better at certain things than others? Are people born with super-hero skills, or just born lucky? Why are some practitioners so much more successful than others? Where does their ever-increasing never-ending queue of clients come from? Do the rich really get richer and the poor get poorer?

We all know someone who, whatever they do, it turns to success, money and happiness. They don't seem any different to anyone else, so how do they do it?

The answer is they have belief. They truly believe they can achieve fantastic results and success is simply a given. Self-doubt, worry, never enters their mind. Their internal subliminal blueprint exudes confidence and achievement. Failure doesn't exist

We all have the same potential

It's true there are huge inequalities in this world. Some people are handed opportunities that others can only dream about. Some of us went to university and got a masters degree, while others left school at 16 without any qualifications. The 1% have massive financial advantages that the rest of us will never enjoy. Regardless of this, we were all born with the same potential.

Confidence and self-belief are at the core of every top performer. They truly believe in themselves, their capabilities, their vision of personal success. To them it's just a matter of time before they get what they want. They think about it every day, visualise themselves in the job they want or driving the car they dream of. The conscious mind convinces the unconscious mind that this is possible over a period of time in such a prolonged and meaningful way that their initial vision becomes a reality.

Achieving unlimited success

How do you get that? The answer is in convincing your conscious mind that you have the ability to achieve your goals. You do this by doing something every day to help you tap into your potential.

Daily rituals, visualising your success, positive meditation on your goals and dreams all help. But you must do at least one thing every day to take you closer to achieving your goals. Accept you can't do it all at once, but as long as you are making progress and your mindset is shifting, you will get there.

The more you believe, the more resourceful you become, the more action you take and your performance improves. The less you believe, the less action you take, the worse your results and performance get. When your performance drops, the less you believe, the less action you take, and your performance gets even worse. And so it continues, a downward spiral supported by doubt and the self-fulfilling prophecy of "Oh well, I did say it might never work."

Take yourself mentally back to a time when you achieved tremendous success, a real Wow! moment when you felt really good and proud of what you had achieved. Go back to that very moment when you first experienced the sense of total self-belief. Total self-certainty and confidence. You are there. This is the difference in people who succeed and people who fail - that certainty.

If you have achieved once, you will achieve again. And it doesn't matter what your achievement was, whether it was "small" and insignificant to others doesn't matter – the important thing is that it was a big success for you. You felt it.

This technique is so simple that people walk right past it. Yet professional sportspeople will pay thousands of pounds to be walked through this exercise. How many famous sportsmen and women can you think of that had it last year but for some reason have lost it now? This is a huge crisis for someone whose livelihood and whole sense of self demands that stay at the top. When helping these individuals the single best way is to help them replay, remember and re-experience those times when they've been hugely successful. Then they get back in the zone, back into that mental state they experienced when they were at the peak of their powers. With enough practice, they can access those associated feelings of confidence, power and competence whenever they need to.

The Success Cycle

Potential = Action = Results = Belief. And so on. The more you believe, the more you tap into your potential, the more action you take and the results improve. As results improve this reinforces your beliefs and confidence, the more motivated you become, the more action you take and the results continue to improve. And on it goes.

This was all brought home to us by Mark's good friend and client Paul McBride, a professional MMA (Mixed Martial Arts) fighter who always seemed to vanish before every fight. When his friends asked him where he disappeared to, he simply replied: "I go somewhere special to train".

Three months leading up to a world title fight his whole world would change. His daily routine, training schedule, diet and - most importantly - his mental application changed dramatically. The secret that eluded his friends and family when they wondered where he disappeared to for three months before every fight was simple. He went somewhere special in his head.

In his mind he created this unbeatable, unstoppable fighting machine, which he subsequently became. He achieved this through daily meditation, rituals and exercises. His mental training reinforced his beliefs and confidence and he did become unstoppable. His entire subliminal internal footprint oozed self-belief and confidence. He won the WKA world kickboxing title three years on the trot.

So decide what you want and commit to doing something different every day towards your goal. Work to achieve that peak mental state; enter the zone and see what you are capable of. Think of the unlimited improvement and results you could achieve by implementing this philosophy in your practice and everyday life.

"Make it so today is not like yesterday and tomorrow will be different forever." - Anthony Robbins, world's number 1 modeller of success and unparalleled NLP life coach: www.tonyrobbins.com

4   The power of confidence

Confidence comes from personal belief. Here's a personal story from Mark about when he learnt this principle for the first time.

"'Success is 90% confidence', said the captain of EnglandRugby as he glanced at me across the table.

"That glance and those words would change my life forever. 'Success is 90% confidence'. These words of wisdom from Will Carling have resonated within me and all the work that I have done with my clients and students ever since.

"At the age of 22, Will was England's youngest ever rugby captain and led the team to their most successful period ever - the World Cup final in 1991. In fact, it was that final he had in mind when he continued his story. 'We were 100% confident we would reach the final', he said, 'but when we got there we had not prepared and therefore lacked confidence and focus to actually win the game'.

"The lesson learnt by his team was that success is down to 90% confidence. So, if you truly believe you can win, with the right preparation and focus you will increase your chances many times over.

At the time they were so focused and confident of getting to the final, they didn't know what to do once they got there.

"That story always stuck in my mind. The more I thought about it the more it made sense. The more I prepared and focused the more confident I became. The more confident I became the more successful I became. The more successful I became the more naturally everything seemed to flow and so it went on...

"I was lucky enough to personally witness this philosophy being echoed by other sporting greats, such as Roger Black, Olympic Games silver medallist and European champion in the 400 metres, and European champion hurdler Chris Akabusi.

"They had similar stories to tell and similar results in evidence. Now many years on, I have to say that success is, without doubt, 90% due to confidence. I embrace this philosophy in every aspect of my life and with all clients that I see in my clinic and achieve wonderful results."

Strategies to build confidence

Confidence, self-esteem and self-belief are at the heart of every success and every failure. Some of us have got it, some of us haven't. Some people can stand and present in front of a large group and many of us shake and are terrified at the prospect of being centre stage. So, what is it that creates or limits our ability?

Confidence or the lack of it is probably responsible for the majority of our successes and failures; it most definitely limits many individuals in their quest to run a vibrant and successful practice. In fact many of life's opportunities are missed or go unexplored due to our inability to even check them out in the first place – due to lack of confidence.

The coaching term for this is "limiting beliefs" or "limiting statements". We focus on what we cannot do, rather than what we can do. A lack of confidence goes hand in hand with low self-esteem and a lack of self-belief. Rather than worry about what may never happen, we need to be able to reframe that and focus on how you will feel once you have explored and embraced those new ideas to take your practice or business to another level.

Our thoughts affect our confidence

How we think and process information is key to our overall levels of confidence and self-esteem. Naturally, if we are positive and upbeat this is reflected in how we feel and subsequently behave.

This is the Cognitive Thinking Cycle. This principle embraces a very simple set of dynamics. What you think impacts how you feel, and impacts how you perform. Simple, isn't it? Therefore if you focus on the positive of every situation rather than the negative you will achieve better results.

Self-esteem

People with high self-esteem generally feel good about themselves. They like and believe in who they are. They feel they are worthy of being happy and successful. They also understand that not everyone is perfect and they can forgive themselves when they make mistakes.

People with high self-esteem experience and enjoy all that life has to offer. When our self-esteem is strong we handle the challenges of life differently.

Low self-esteem sufferers see themselves as negative, destructive, and limited. They are often vulnerable, withdrawn and insecure. They are unable to find a positive edge on anything and are particularly self-critical.

Self-confidence

Self confidence is the energy that is created by your self-esteem and belief. People with high self-confidence have an underlying self-belief in all that they do. These people accept they are good at some things and not so good at others and they accept themselves and are happy and content with all that they have.

Self-acceptance

To raise your self-esteem and confidence you first have to accept and embrace who and what you are. A good starting point is to accept you cannot be great at everything, and acknowledge the things you are good at. The aim here is to align your actions and results with your personal values and beliefs.

Feedback, not failure

We've already established the NLP presupposition that there is no failure, only feedback. It may sound impractical to say failure doesn't exist. But the mental and emotional attitude behind this is important. For example, if you complete a consultation that was difficult and did not go at all to plan, you have a clear choice. You can rack it up as a "failure" and beat yourself up about it, or you can look upon this as a learning experience, a "teaching moment". Then ask for and give yourself feedback. "What did I learn from this experience?" "What could I have done differently?" "If faced with this again how would I change things?"

Ask for feedback from clients on a regular basis, especially when you are concerned that things didn't go quite right. How can we improve our practices and practitioner skills if we don't know where we are going wrong in the first place?

The thing is that "feedback" is interpreted far more easily than "failure". Our minds regard failure as limiting and final. Thoughts of failure drag us down and affect our self-esteem and subsequently our confidence. Concerns that we might fail AGAIN are more toxic to our performance.

Feedback can nullify that. Take the feedback, learn what to do differently next time, and we are not only not going to fail, we are actually going to improve.Our confidence and self-belief will soar.

Knowledge is power

It is what we learn every day that helps us build long term to a more profitable and sustainable practice.

But it is a common trap to rate your personal success instead by what's been achieved: for example, how many clients seen, how busy the practice is. This is a common trap and one which a lot of us fall into.

Remember the adage "Knowledge is Power". Apply this and reframe. Judge and value yourself by what you learn from your experience in practice as opposed to what you achieve.

Look at every experience or period in your life and judge this period not by how much money you earned, but by how much you learned. Obviously money is important but the balance should be weighted by the value of knowledge and experience gained, rather than anything else.

Getting back into the Zone

Revisit some of your past successes, perhaps when you first started out as a practitioner and achieved your first success with a client, or when you had a great day in the student clinic. What was that like?

Allow yourself to recapture those feelings when sitting quietly and reflecting on all the value-adding work you have done with people in the past just to bring those success anchors back to the surface and allow you to reinforce how good and capable you really are.

Confidence does breed success. And high levels of confidence, self-belief, and enthusiasm are contagious.

Your clients, business partners, suppliers and everyone you deal with will notice.

Having the power to inspire everyone around you can only impact on your life and business in a positive way.

Practitioner Case Study

5 Hot Tips for Running the Perfect Practice
- Rebecca Smith

Some of you reading this book will be thinking of setting up a business in the complementary therapy world, just as I was nearly 20 years ago. I know just how you feel. All those years later and here I am, having been in continual practice since gaining my first qualification in Systematic Kinesiology. Over the years I have added extra skills to my practice - Hypnotherapy, NLP, EFT and Life Coaching, which allow me to offer an integrated service to clients, aiming to deliver an excellent client experience to all who come through the door.

The business that I now co-own with my partner, who practises as a remedial masseur and osteomyologist, runs under the banner of Newport Complementary Health Clinic in a small Shropshire market town. Together we have successfully set up and maintained a profitable practice through several difficult economic climates and we are busier than ever. We started from very humble beginnings and have grown into the established clinic that we always dreamed of.

The rarity of our success was recently pointed out to me when I was working with Mark Shields of Life Practice UK, who reminded me of the poor statistics that have been discussed in this book: only 5% in the complementary health industry achieve success in business. Mark was interested to know how we have achieved and sustained our success in the marketplace for so many years, and asked me to share my top 5 tips.

My tips are in no particular order of importance and are what I consider to have been the most important in our continuing success.

1. Client Commitment

A successful Complementary Health business relies on a two-way relationship between you the practitioner (seller) and the client (buyer). It doesn't take too much effort to get a client to visit your clinic once; it's the repeat business that can be a little trickier.Reputation is everything in this business, and what your clients think of you and your skills can either make or break a business. With this in mind, I feel that it is up to us as therapists who are aiming to help a person feel better in some way, to set high standards of commitment to clients, ensuring that every time we interact with them, face to face or other, you give them an excellent experience that meets their expectations and their needs.

Your client's needs must be a top priority and as it's such a simple area to address for establishing and maintaining a profitable business, that many practitioners overlook it. Be committed to helping them in the best way that you can, respect them and value them.These people are your livelihood, do a good job and they will tell everyone they know about you, and they will think of you in the future over and above everyone else if ever they need help. Without them, you have no income.

Treat everyone as you would expect to be treated yourself and you can't go far wrong. Time and time again, experience has proven to me that honesty is always the best policy. You can't help everyone, so don't be afraid to refer a client on or to have an honest discussion when you think things may not be going as you had hoped. If you are asked a question and you don't know the answer, say "I don't know, but I can find out for you". The client will ALWAYS appreciate your honesty. I have had occasions where having had a consultation with the client, it is clear that I'm not the right person to help and I have referred them on to someone else. Those clients have then gone on to recommend me, even though I never actually treated them.

My experience tells me that this is such an important area to address, yet sadly overlooked by many practitioners. These are my Top 10 Tips for Client Commitment

1. Keep to time, never be late and never cancel an appointment once agreed.
2. Be polite and respectful. If a client introduces themselves as Mr or Mrs, address them in that way until you have asked permission if you can call them by their Christian name.
3. Remain non-judgemental ALWAYS. They are not the problem, the problem is the problem.
4. Be professional and maintain healthy client boundaries. Adhere to ethical standards and stick to strict codes of conduct.
5. Confidentiality is key. Reassure the client, especially if they have been recommended or you are practising in a small town, that everything they tell you remains confidential. Never gossip about clients.
6. Go the extra mile for them and "be the difference that makes the difference". Let them know that you will take an action to help them too.
7. As a health professional, look after your own health and work on balancing your own life, mentally and physically. A client presenting to you with issues of stress and exhaustion will not respect a practitioner who is yawning and complaining how tired they are. Equally, a client is presenting with issues of poor health and is going to be looking for inspiration from you. Embody a way of being and a lifestyle that you are asking your clients to embrace. Each time you give them a piece of advice, check to ensure that you are heeding the advice too. They will admire a practitioner who clearly "practises what they preach".

8. Be reliable and consistent. Always do what you say you will do. Forgetting is unforgiveable.
9. Dress appropriately. Think about the message you want to convey to your client when they first meet you. Your visual image will convey a lot to that new client.
10. Above all, be enthusiastic! Listen to the client, let them know that they are really important, make them feel valued, that you really care about their issues and reassure them that you can help. Give them an experience, not an explanation. Empower them while they are in your company and give them an experience that they can take away with them and remember.

We owe it to our clients to be on top of our game, personally and professionally. It's always the simplest aspects of a business that get overlooked, yet these aspects are often among the most important.

2. Update your learning

Whether you have one discipline to your name or several, a good understanding of your subject is very important if you are to be successful in business. Set your standards high and commit to regular learning and development. A growing business relies upon you to continue your professional development (CPD), acquiring new skills and keeping up to date with current practices.

Many professional associations stipulate regular CPD training as a requirement for acknowledgement as a member. While for some, the thought of extra tuition may make you groan, as it takes time and money, it's really worth remembering the commitment that you have made to your clients. To do the very best that you can to deliver a unique experience that no one else is offering, means you need to update regularly. New learning brings new life and energy into a business and prevents you from becoming stagnant and outdated as a practitioner. You will gain respect from being ahead in your game.

These days, you do not even need to leave the comfort of your home or office to complete CPD hours. Many companies now offer webinars, where you take part in a live event on all aspects of complementary health from nutrition to muscular-skeletal techniques and functional health testing, for example. Many associations offer cost-effective ways to add to your existing knowledge on a subject.Or, of course, you can go the whole hog and re-train in a totally new therapy that you feel your business would benefit from.

Each and every session with a client is a potential learning experience. After they leave the session, ask yourself, "What have I learnt from that?'" This type of learning allows you to refine the service that you offer to future clients. All learning is positive.

In my clinic, my CPD certificates are available for clients to view, allowing them to see that I am prepared to go the extra mile for them and that they can benefit from any new learning that I receive. This makes the client feel that I genuinely have their best interests at heart and that the sessions that I deliver to them are very important to me.Complementary Health relies on a two-way relationship; this kind of action from you, the practitioner, helps to cement your client's trust in you.

The amount and type of training is often up to you, but something that I would wholeheartedly recommend. Empower yourself with new skills and knowledge, without stretching yourself too thin. A prospective client may be a little put off if you offer them 20 therapies to choose from. Stick to a couple of core subjects and just add complementary skills to those.

If you are reading this and it's been a while since you've done something different, or if you feel your business is stale and not moving with the times, then do something new today. Take action and let your clients know about it. Be willing to fill in the gaps of your knowledge. The potential benefits and rewards to you both could be just what your business needs right now.

3. Manage budgets and costs

Having a structured approach to your business is most important if you are to maintain a smooth running, profitable practice. Part of this structure is managing the costs of running that business. Costs involved in a business concern your income from clients' sessions and other products that you may sell, amenities of the building, such as heating, lighting etc, equipment, advertising, accountant's fees, income tax, VAT, CPD training fees and insurance, to name a few.

My best tip: keep it simple in the beginning. Make a list of all the necessities and stick to that. Only spend what you have now; branch out and grow as the business becomes financially viable. Clients pay to see you. Having them sit in an elaborate waiting room will make them wonder if their money is being spent on their time with you, or just to fund the lavish surroundings!

Once you have decided on your fees, decide how many clients you need to see a week to realistically earn what you want. This will allow you to begin to understand how much money there will be to spend in the business, firstly on necessities and only later, in those other areas.

In the beginning, only pay for what you really need. Keeping overheads low and the business plan simple means fewer costs for you while establishing the business. For example, buy secondhand equipment and books and, if in your own building, shop around for the best prices on gas and electric supplies. It really does make a difference. The same advice goes for accountants and malpractice insurance companies; prices vary enormously. Choose the company that can offer you what you need as a new business. Do your homework before you even open the doors to that first client.

Negotiate a fair deal on the rent of the building or therapy room, explaining that you are new in business. Many properties/therapy rooms are empty and you will find a landlord only too happy to have a regular paying tenant. After a set time, agree that the rent can be sensibly reviewed and the agreement lengthened.

If your business involves selling products, keep stock very low, unless you can sell it daily. For those practitioners using nutritional supplements, nearly all companies now provide a patient ordering system where the client orders the supplements for themselves and you are acknowledged with commission. This means that virtually no outlay needs to be allocated to keep stock, which is costly to any business, new or old.

Be choosy how you spend money on advertising. In this climate, allocate nearly all your budget to website advertising, as has been mentioned in this book. Writing a column in a local monthly magazine has provided me with a regular presence in my small town, with readers following my articles on various aspects of health. Often, placing a regular advert will grant you free editorial space, with the added bonus (in a monthly publication) that these tend to hang around in people's houses for the month until the next edition arrives. Weekly publications are usually put out for recycling within a few days. All readers are prospective clients and they will value interesting articles that relate to them, rather than those that are blatant advertising of your business. I have had clients attend an appointment having followed my column for 2 years before deciding to pick up the phone.All articles can be added to your website, providing a section of current interest, helping you gain Internet presence.

The costs in my business have been successfully managed by the principles above, with a degree of commonsense and simplicity.Living within my means has meant starting small and branching out as and when finances of the business have allowed. I have never employed a receptionist, explaining on my website and to all enquirers the procedure to follow when they come to the clinic. I use an answerphone when I am with clients and ALWAYS respond to all enquiries within less than 24 hours. I have set my days and hours of work and am in charge of my own diary, giving me total control, allowing no room for error. I am solely responsible for the running of my business, the only outside help coming from a trusted accountant, meaning I can keep all costs very low.

Never become complacent about the costs of running your business. The ever-changing economic climate can be difficult to negotiate, so remaining focused and attentive to the needs of the business is vital.

4. Keep up to date

As the world that we live in is ever-changing, so are the needs of the clients that are presenting to a Complementary Health practitioner.The problems and issues that clients presented with 20 years ago are very different to those of now. Stress, for example, was mentioned far less frequently back then, whereas now almost every client will speak of feeling stressed in one way or another. Offering advice, support and programmes that address the current needs of clients in a fast moving world can set you apart from others.

Entering into your client's map of thinking, means you can see the world through their eyes, gaining insight into what it is they need from you. Do your homework into what the client wants and expects. Don't be frightened to ask for feedback. What a client needs from you is really important and their comments allow you to take an honest, objective look at your practice, ensuring you can offer what they are asking for. It may be that you have to consider the time constraints a client may have and offer telephone consultations, or Skype sessions.Instead of 3 sessions to work on a problem, you may need to offer a longer appointment across the whole day, allowing the client to address their issue without the need for further disruption to an already stressed life. Or it may be that you choose to travel to them for their session.

If your discipline involves recommending products and supplements to clients, offer to order them for the client, saving them the need to have to do that themselves. Offer to take the pressure off them and show them that you are prepared to do something extra to help.

Keeping up to date also means employing methods of technology without which a business can very soon be left behind. Involvement with Skype, websites, Twitter, Facebook etc will ensure that a business moves with the times and can offer the very best to all clients that ask for help.

There are many ways to remain informed on current topics, among the simplest is to read relevant, up to date information. Monthly publications, books and the Internet offer a wealth of material to the reader, an easy way to add information to your current knowledge. Regular attendance on CPD training courses shows a desire to learn for the benefit of the client and allows you to grow as a practitioner. Without new skills and information, you cannot move forward and you cannot sustain success.

Think about the current climate that we live in and consider the problems and dilemmas your presenting clients are facing. Imagine their world for a while if you are to offer them very best help that you can.

5. Location, location

One of the most important considerations of being successful in any business is the location. As reputation is key in a Complementary Health business, starting in a small location while building a credible reputation has been successful for me. Working in one location initially allows people in the local area to get to know of your regular presence.

If all of your working hours are based in this one place, prospective clients are more likely to hear your name mentioned over and over again, in different circles. This then gives them some reassurance that if two of their friends and the lady on the supermarket checkout have mentioned your name, then you must be worth a visit. It can often take a client months or even years to make the initial enquiry to you, so knowing that you have a good reputation in your local area will often secure the appointment.

There are other advantages to keeping to one location while you build your business. Local GPs, gym owners, other complementary health therapists and so on will all hear about you and what you do. These networks of professionals are a potential source of referrals to your business and being part of a team, with skills that complement yours, means that you can ask for extra support and advice if needed. A community of therapists in a small area can be an attraction to potential clients.

A primary location also allows you to assist your client in their journey to you. Learning train routes, bus timetables and various road routes means you can give client "idiot proof" directions to reach you, helping them to make their appointment on time. Working with a client who is late and flustered will result in a rushed and difficult session. Help your clients in all ways that you can to locate your practice easily and effortlessly.

Once successful and you have a good reputation locally, branch out if necessary to other towns. If you spread yourself too thin by spending only half a day a week in different towns, not many people get to know that you are there and your business goes unnoticed. You will find that once your name has been established, people will travel to you from all parts of the country and even from around the world.

A winning strategy

This book has provided the grim statistics of the amount of practitioners who are actually making a success in the business of Complementary and Alternative Medicine. Most of my top 5 tips are rooted in commonsense and are what I consider to be important considerations in becoming and remaining successful in business. I work the hours that I want, earn a living that is acceptable to me and most of all, enjoy every day that I work at my clinic.

Build your practice around your strengths and find out what works for your business and stick to it. Take action every week to market your business, aiming to ensure a steady stream of clients, new and old. You really can make your own luck, don't wait for someone else to initiate the idea that you've been sitting on.

Some sessions with clients will be textbook, some may be a little sticky, but there is always something positive to learn from each and every experience that you have with a client.

Always endeavour to do your best and you can't go far wrong.

The best advice I was given when I started out was to have faith, confidence and belief in your products and your services, because the main reason people contact you is that they have lost their faith, confidence and belief in other peoples' products and services.

Rebecca Smith, Systematic Kinesiologist, Hypnotherapist, NLP Master Practitioner, Proprietor of the Newport Complementary Health Clinic, Newport, Shropshire: www.newportcomplementaryhealthclinic.co.uk

Chapter 7: Attracting and retaining quality clients

A typical client has been ill for a while. They've done the rounds of GP and whatever else the NHS has to offer and are still unwell. They then spend weeks or months wondering whether some form of CAM might help, then researching it. They may even have tried one or more practitioners before you.

Now they're back on the Internet looking for your particular therapy somewhere convenient. They're looking for a practitioner who looks right. Finally they find your website. They email you; maybe they even phone the practice. So in total it may have taken your prospective client several months to pluck up the courage to turn to another practitioner, then go through the whole selection process.

What do you think will happen to that client, or more importantly how will that client feel, if after making contact, either filling in your contact form on your website, or phoning you directly, they fail to get a response?

According to a 2009 survey of 7,000 patients by Reva Health, that's just what happened to more than a quarter of people contacting private health clinics. While a staggering 88% of client/patient contact requests were handled in an unacceptable manner, amazingly that figure includes 28% of enquires that were never answered at all! Reva Health is a branch of a branch of www.whatclinic.com, a search engine and consumer survey outfit dedicated to reviewing health clinics of all stripes. Their findings are so surprising, that we're quoting their report at length here. They have some suggestions to make; we have what we think is a better answer, which we'll explain after this report from Reva.

28% of online patient enquiries go unanswered

"More than a quarter of patients who use the Internetto contact health clinics are reporting that they never receive a reply, and a full 60% claim that their enquiry was not responded to in an effective manner.

"These are the shocking results of a survey of over 7,000 patients carried out during 2009 by leading healthcare search engine RevaHealth.com. The main reasons cited by patients for why they weren't happy with the responses they did receive were:

- The clinic took too long to respond
- The response itself was unprofessional
- The patient never received a follow-up phone call

"Patients also indicated that:

- They expect an instant automatic response to confirm receipt of their enquiry
- They want to be told when they should expect a personal call or email response
- They expect that personal response by the end of the next working day

"Clinics that don't meet these expectations risk losing the patient as a paying customer. To find out why clinics were falling so far short of meeting patients' expectations, RevaHealth.com also surveyed 30 health clinics and asked them what problems they were facing.

Why do clinics find it hard to cope?

"The single biggest problem reported by clinics was that they didn't have the resources to deal with email enquiries in a timely fashion. Other daily tasks and issues often took precedence and often there was no single person responsible for looking after the clinic's email account, meaning emails got lost or ignored regularly.

"This same lack of resources led to poor follow-up procedures. Rather than making phone calls to patients who hadn't yet committed, clinics were waiting for them to call back themselves.

"The next biggest problem was that the clinics were experiencing technical problems but didn't have permanent staff who could resolve the issues. Sometimes emails to customers would bounce back to the clinic and no one would contact the customer to correct the mistake. Other times, their contact form would break and they wouldn't know who to contact to get it fixed.

Why are patients increasingly turning to the internet?

"The Internet is the fastest growing source of health information, with patients enjoying the convenience of access to information 24/7 from the comfort and privacy of their own homes. The ability to research treatment options, read other patients' reviews, and compare clinics' prices means that more and more patients are starting their health research online.

"A recent analysis of user behavior by RevaHealth.com showed that

*51% of patients chose to contact a clinic using their email enquiry form
* 45% chose to look up the phone number from a website and
* 4% did both.

"Clinics without an email enquiry form for patients are clearly running the risk of losing a large proportion of their potential customers.

"The same behavior analysis also turned up the fact that patients on average look up 1.4 phone numbers and email 1.8 clinics, ie patients are often contacting more than one clinic and deciding where to seek treatment based on the responses they receive.

How can clinics meet these new expectations using current resources?

"There is no one easy answer to this question, but the simplest one is that clinics need to get smarter about using the many cheap or free online tools available to them. Nowadays, even a small business can access much of the same technology as large corporations.

"There is no need to pay lots of money anymore for someone to provide your clinic with email. Google can do it for next to nothing, and with probably the most extensive network of servers on the planet, their service hardly ever fails. It can even handle automatic responses and stock replies.

"Industry specific services like those on RevaHealth.com or more generic services like HighriseHQ.com and Remember TheMilk.com allow clinic staff to organize their schedules and set reminders for calls and emails in one place. They can even send reminders to staff members' mobile phones if needs be, meaning they don't even have to be by the computer to get a reminder.

"Clinics should also give one person overall responsibility for online enquiries. This doesn't mean they have to handle all the enquiries, but it does mean they're responsible for monitoring how many they receive, and how many of these turn into patients. This attention to details should mean that problems in a clinic's sales process become clear very quickly.

"While these steps might be a burden at first, they should lead to a streamlined and efficient system of dealing with and converting patient enquiries into paying customers, and that is something that every clinic big or small should be interested in achieving".

(Press release from Reva Health: www.revahealth.com)

• **Why you need service level agreements**

Not responding to client enquiries in a timely, structured and professional way is business suicide and clinics that can't get this right often don't last very long. You need to have a plan, and the formal name for that plan is a Service Level Agreement, or SLA.

An SLA is a level of service you promise and commit to as a minimum standard for your business. An SLA is a promise from a practitioner to all potential clients.

An SLA dealing with client contact and response is normally found on the contact page of websites can look like this:

1. We are committed to providing a world-class service to all our clients.
2. We promise to reply to any email enquiry in writing within 24 hours of receipt.
3. We promise to return any phone call within the same business day.
4. We will see you at a time convenient to you during the day, evening or weekend, subject to clinic opening times as found on our website.
5. We guarantee to offer you an appointment within seven days of your initial enquiry.
6. If your enquiry is urgent we guarantee to offer you an appointment within 48 hours of your enquiry.
7. We will communicate with you via your preferred communication method whether it is face to face, Skype, email, or phone, outside of your booked appointment times.

8. We offer a 24-hour 24/7 response line for all urgent client requirements.

This is almost identical to the client commitment statement Mark issued on his first practice website. Up front for all to see. "I never broke an SLA and I never have to this day", he says.Other areas of your business where it is sensible to use SLAS are

- Invoicing and payment
- Client confidentiality
- Data marketing
- Business partner communication
- Room hire
- Product sale and return

Treat your clients like royalty. They are the ones who are important. Treat them well and you will receive more referrals than you can handle. By having clear Service Level Agreements in place you deliver on the vision and mission of your practice and clients know where they stand. You will deliver a first-class, transparent service. Display your SLAs prominently on your website, as it will help you stand out from the competition.

Mark's Modelling Tip

Your response time for every client interaction or contact request must be immediate, decisive, structured and certainly must happen within 24 hours - at the latest. If you can't get this bit of your business correct you may as well stop right now.

• The Secret of Attraction

We have already made the point that around 50% of CAM practitioners don' t go into practice upon qualifying. We also know the failure rate in the early years in the complementary and alternative medicine market is far higher than in general business.

Research suggests that 10% of CAM practitioners practise full-time and 33% of this 10% earn a comfortable living. You don't need to be a genius to do the maths. So the message is clear. Lots of us want to go into private practice and half actually do. Of that half a third go full time and around 10% make a comfortable living.

It is surprising how much opportunity goes untapped due to practitioners' lack of business acumen. Which is why we are here. This is so often coupled with issues around charging clients and also setting expectations about how many clients they hoped to see each week.

The equations are simple enough. The amount you charge reflects the value you put on yourself and if you are serious, then you must remember that this is now your livelihood. The number of clients you expect to see each week is worked out in line with your business and marketing plans with one objective in mind: to deliver a certain amount of income.

The secret is in how to make sure your practice is busy, attracting and sustaining quality clients month after month. Consistency and sustainability is key. The practitioners who come for coaching do want to be successful and earn a comfortable living, but genuinely don't know how. Attracting the right type of client, the right number of clients on a daily basis is key. As a practitioner you have to adopt a focused, disciplined approach to ensuring your clinic is full.

1. How many clients do you need?

Forecast how much income you want to earn and divide this number by 45 weeks – a reasonable amount of working weeks, allowing for sickness and holidays. Calculate your average income per client session. Divide your annual income forecast by this average client spend. This will give you the total amount of client visits you need annually to achieve your earnings target.

Simply going through this process and forming a written plan will add to your focus and help you attract more clients. Remember the Harvard MBAs! Write down your goals!

2. Adopt a professional approach

However small you think your business, adopt a professional approach and never compromise your image or reputation. Remember, "You are what you are perceived to be."

Your reputation is the most important thing you have, never compromise it. This starts with your website. It must be professional. It is your showcase to the world. Whether you believe it or not, if you are going to be a professional practitioner you have to have a professional web presence.

Also, in this day and age you need to be able to deal with client requirements at all levels of demand. Make sure you have a credit card machine, for example. 78% more clients want to pay in this way. If you can't offer this facility you can't compete. (You can get a good credit card machine from CardSave for around £15 per month: www.cardsave. net)

Don't advertise your mobile phone number unless your business is mobile. A landline is far more professional and gives the impression you are stable. Your landline number will also let people know you are local.

3. The secret of successful advertising

Set an advertising budget and you stick to it. Make sure you are spending enough (see chapter 5). Use Google AdWords. By allocating a small budget and cleverly timing your campaign you can turn the tap on to a steady flow of enquiries whenever you want or need to. It's that simple.

Start your campaign at 4pm every day. This will allow your competitor's budgets to expire and you will reach number one on Google at half the normal price. In addition the evening is the most popular viewing time, so you'll get double the viewings for half the cost.

4. Obtaining referrals

The best business is referred business. Don't be afraid to ask; your competitors will. Give every new client a business card and leaflet. Leave something visual with them to put on the fridge or in their wallet. You don't want them to forget you.

There are many techniques about asking for referrals. The "specifically for you" technique is as good as any I know and goes a little like this.

"As we are going through this process together, as it's personal and about you, I'm sure other people will come to mind in a similar situation or with similar needs. Don't worry, when we are finished I will remind you of this and give you some business cards to give them or I will take their details and contact them". Don't be afraid. Good clients know it's tough out there at the moment and they will help you if they can.

Keep your newsletter going out regularly and keep getting email addresses and permission to build your subscriber base. Even if readers don't book for themselves, if you are keeping them informed and giving them good value they will become another source of referrals.

5. Create your own PR

Local businesses like to support local businesses. Approach the local paper for editorial, or the local radio to give advice on your particular therapy. If you don't ask you don't get.

Approach the local gym to put up a poster of what you do, or the local doctor's surgery or dentist's. Local community magazines are excellent. They cost around £20 to advertise in and reach in excess of 1000 people all living and working within a mile of you.

These techniques are modelled on success. They work and are currently working for other people; why shouldn't they work for you?

• How to Respond to an Enquiry: The 3-Step Process

This is a simple yet very effective way of booking in new clients after they have contacted you.

You'll see "the difference that makes the difference" quite easily here, and it builds on two things we already know: first, the often lengthy and emotional process your prospective client has gone through before getting in touch with you, and second, that rapport is the key to building a relationship. Let's look at this in the form of a case study.

Richard is 27 years old and has suffered with mild stress-related depression for about three months. He's finally seen his GP, with encouragement from family and friends to "get help", and the doctor has suggested Richard tries adopting life-style changes and possibly sees a professional practitioner before trying medication.

Richard goes online and completes enquiry forms on four practitioners' websites. You are the fourth he emailed. His email arrives at 8pm on a Friday night after you've got home from work.

What would you do now?

Be honest. How would you handle that enquiry; when and how would you respond; and what are your chances of turning Richard into a client? Write down your answer.

This is how it works, and how Mark teaches it.

Step 1   **Acknowledge and respond**

Always carry a mobile phone/iPad that has an electronic version of your diary on it and enables you to pick up emails. Assuming you check your phone for emails every hour or so, email a confirmation response immediately. In Richard's case this is going out around 9pm or 10pm on Friday night. Give him the option to take a call from you within the next 24 hours – suggest 11am the next morning - so you can discuss his requirements in more detail.

This lets him know you have received his enquiry and – Wow! You've responded immediately, even late on a Friday night. You really do look like a practitioner who puts their clients first. He confirms he can talk to you. After waiting months, Richard now has an appointment to speak with you in person at 11am. He can relax and talk at his own pace as it's a Saturday morning.

Step 2   **Your 30-minute free initial consultation**

Call Richard promptly at 11am as arranged. Allow at least 30 minutes for the call and tell Richard you offer a free initial 30-minute telephone consultation and ask him if he would like to conduct that now. (In the majority of cases the client will take you up on this offer, if not you simply re- appoint for a more convenient time.)

This session really helps you understand their specific needs and lets you begin to give some thought about how you might help them. Very importantly from your perspective it gives you the opportunity to build high levels of rapport and get to know your future client.

During this conversation you need to ensure three things happen:

1. You are genuinely interested in Richard's requirements.
2. Reassure Richard you can help and he will be fine.
3. Explain you are running a very busy practice, however due to his circumstances you will fit him in, even if it has to be over the weekend or late in the evening.
A little reverse psychology always helps, as it is human nature to want what you can't have. When your practice is busy, the perception is that you must be good at what you do and it adds to your credibility.

Most importantly you have just spent a valuable 30 minutes building rapport. In any sales or service industry rapport is key in establishing trust and relaxing your client, enabling them to make sensible decisions. Also you have had 30 minutes to sell yourself and your services to Richard, with no hurry and no pressure, and within 24 hours of his initial enquiry. How powerful is that?

Step 3   Offer something for free
During your consultation you will be continually building rapport and listening to him. Give him some free tips as you speak: strategies to help him immediately, perhaps some recommended reading to help him understand his situation better, or something he can buy or some exercises he can do, to help him before he sees you.

In addition ask him to drop you an email with a full description of his situation as he sees it, including a full time line to show when he first started experiencing stress and depression symptoms. Explain that this information will help you prepare for your session together and you can then spend the full hour working on helping him rather than on basic fact-finding.

Following on the free stuff and the homework, you are going to ask for the appointment.

"How urgently would you like to be seen? As it's urgent Richard, I can fit you in next Thursday at 10am or Friday evening at 7pm. If it can wait and isn't so urgent, how about a week on Wednesday at 10am, or a week on Thursday at 5pm?"

If you follow this process exactly and each step goes according to plan, you'll have secured Richard as a client and have your first appointment booked.

Imagine if you used this technique with every enquiry. Once you had mastered each step you could be confident of achieving a practitioner proficiency rate of enquiry to appointment of 100%. Imagine what that would do for your practice. You would simply then need to review your strategy of getting clients to your website and through to the enquiry stage; because once they enquired you would be completely confident in securing an appointment.

Richard's other three emails

Richard emailed four practitioners, you were the fourth. This is what happened with the other three.

Enquiry 1: Practitioner waited until their practice was open again and called Richard at 2pm Monday afternoon.

Enquiry 2: Practitioner responded immediately to Richard, thanking him for his enquiry and confirmed she would be in touch the following week to make an appointment.

Enquiry 3: Practitioner picked up the enquiry from Richard on Monday and acknowledged his email, asking him to contact the practice to make an appointment

So who won the client? Remember this is what most clients go through when looking for a practitioner.

Mark has been using this three-step approach for six years and his enquiry to appointment rate is 98%. He teaches this approach on all is courses and when coaching practitioners. In every case performances dramatically improve.

• The importance of targeted marketing

When you go through the process of branding and profiling your business, have a certain type of client in mind: your "ideal client"

Know exactly the type of client you want to work with and adjust your proposition and pricing so that you will attract the exact client you are looking for.

This gives you an element of control over

- How much you can charge
- The amount of sessions you can expect to have with that client
- Referral potential
- Selling your services as a package as opposed to one off ad hoc sessions

Market your proposition in such a way that only the clients you want to attract will contact you. There are different ways of doing this:

1. You would target affluent clients by being the most expensive practitioner in your area.
2. You could offer specialist services on your website, such as stress programmes for executives, or confidence programmes for directors.
3. You could run a specialist health and nutrition programme at your area's most exclusive golf club or resort

Other examples of this are advertising bespoke programmes for

- The entertainment industry
- Professional sports people
- Retiring sportsmen and women
- West End stars
- Services for tv actors and actresses
- Services for celebrities with problems

All of the above would attract a high value, wealthy clientele. Whatever the type of client you're looking to attract you can do it in this way by designing and marketing highly targeted programmes.

• The money thing: charging your clients

So many practitioners, especially when they are just starting out, have challenges with charging their clients realistic fees,

Nearly all of them do get over this. YOU will get over this. The realisation that the value they put on themselves is reflected in their charges is quickly followed by the realisation that a lot of clients know this. Many clients associate ability with money. The more expensive you are, the better you are. And within reason, who doesn't want the best? Your clients definitely do.

What client would want to work with a practitioner who charged middle of the road prices and came across as just about average? Of course, there are inequalities and some people genuinely can't afford top-end fees. It is up to you how you deal with this. By all means have a sliding scale that enables you to see deserving cases at low cost, but don't build your practice around those types of clients and don't advertise your discounted prices.

When practitioners approach Mark for help because business is far from booming and they only have a few clients, the first thing he does is review their pricing structure. Normally he ends up recommending a fee increase of at least 50%, sometimes more. In every case they see an enormous immediate improvement in client footfall. People want the best.

Mark says: "Three years ago I worked with a struggling team of nutritional therapists based in Harley Street. They were on the verge of closing shop as they were averaging, between six of them, just over £1,500 per month

"The first thing I did was double their prices. The very next month I had a phone call from the managing director telling me they had had their best ever month since they started trading some years before and had grossed over £6,000 for the month.

"They were delighted. This change to their pricing structure had increased their business by 400%. When I met them they were seriously considering reducing their prices as they believed this was the reason why they weren't getting enough clients. I've seen this a number of times with different practitioners. Never reduce your prices. It's the beginning of the end if you do."

Part 3: Sustaining a Successful Practice - 6-18 months and Beyond

Chapter 8: Motivational Interviewing

"Of course you can motivate. You can motivate people by being who you are." - Franz Stampfl, MBE, one of the world's most successful multi-sport coaches, advisor to Sir Roger Bannister, first man to run the mile in under four minutes: www.franzthemovie.com

The ability to motivate and inspire your clients is fundamental to the overall commitment you will get from them and ultimately contributes heavily to the success of your sessions.

Failure to motivate and inspire often results in clients dropping out of a programme early and not following through on actions they've agreed with you at the outset. They will cancel or just not turn up for their next appointment. We have all had clients "disappear" on us.

This chapter will explain the skill of motivational interviewing and the impact it can have on empowering the client to achieve the life changes they are looking for. We'll also explore people's natural resistance to change and how to establish where your client is on the "ready to change" scale.

Mark's Modelling Tip

"Your ability to be able to motivate and inspire your client will be the difference that makes the difference in facilitating the results you require with any individual client".

• **Inspiration, Motivation, Procrastination**

How are these linked and what part do they play in the success or failure with our clients?

"Inspiration comes forth from within. It's what the light burning within you is about, as opposed to motivation, which is doing it because if you don't do it, there will be negative repercussions. Motivation is making me do something that I don't really want to do." - Esther Hicks, author "The Law of Attraction".

Procrastination seems to be one of the biggest problems clients experience when embracing change in their lives. There is an entire industry (namely the personal development industry) focused almost entirely on attempting to address this problem, helping us get clear on our goals and then motivating us via all manner of coercion to achieve them.

Guilt, irritation, shame, self-sabotage, stress, the fear of not reaching our potential, anger at self, beating oneself up, right path/wrong path thinking etc all accompany the so-called "unmotivated"client.

One of two things can happen when you find yourself procrastinating or seeking to motivate yourself. You will motivate yourself with head talk and force yourself to do something that most likely does not feel particularly good. Or you can wait (aka procrastinate), until you feel inspired from within to do it. The first, motivation, will take substantial effort, be a fleeting addictive type high followed by a down, feeling like a pat on the back that may leave you wanting. The second, inspiration, takes courage, will feel genuinely good and uplifting, absorbing, purposeful and of course inspired!

A personal note from Mark:

"It's been a journey of many years now to learn to live from inspiration; the most notable experience was when I was a senior bank manager in a previous career. This was a wonderful time for my family and I and we seemed to be riding on the crest of a wave. We had it all. The house on the hill, the sea view and the boat in the harbor, but sadly it did not seem to inspire me.

"I didn't procrastinate for more than a couple of months, as once my mind was made up I was ready to change my life for ever. I felt inspired to become the best Life Coach in the UK. There was an element of fear in this career change as the prestige and kudos in my bank position was what everybody seemed to want, so I had to stay motivated with my new idea.

"I felt inspired and motivated to study in my spare time and took the relevant qualifications; I was itching to see my first client. It just felt better when I thought about life coaching, so I took a deep breath and amicably left the bank. In less than a week I was running my own life coaching practice.

"An internationally acclaimed coach and personal friend told me, "For goodness' sake, Mark, live the dream - you only live once!" I was both motivated and enormously inspired by this statement and his advice helped me leave the safe zone of banking, which was all I had known for 20 years, and the desire to become a famous life coach became my first choice.

"The desire to inspire and motivate people to live the dream within the boundaries of their own goals and dreams was enormously satisfying.

"Again I find myself, as will you, moving into new areas with new inspirations. Perhaps you are bashing your head against what you 'should do' ... outdated ideas and projects that are motivated by living up to some ideal set by someone else, or perhaps doing what you feel you should or ought to be doing in the hope of fantasy rewards at the end of the 'hard slog'.

"It takes courage to live free and in the flow of your own calling - but the reward is extraordinary. I believe that the word inspiration originally means to be filled with life, passion, and emotional and physical balance and wellbeing, achieving great results in your own life and the lives of your patients and clients."

This shows the fundamental differences between inspiration and motivation and also how a lack of motivation is fuelled by procrastination. As practitioners we need to be able to identify our client's levels of procrastination and resistance to change and find ways to inspire them which in turn will motivate them to take action.

As a rule of thumb inspiration is found on the inside, while motivation comes from the outside.

The experience of motivation

1. Are you focused on the outcome of your success with your clients?
2. Do you find yourself comparing the success of your practice to others?
3. Do you ever say, "I know I should be trying that with my clients, but..."?
4. Do you waste a lot of time feeling guilty?
5. Do you achieve goals and then wonder what the point of it was?

The experience of inspiration

1. Do you feel a strong sense of purpose and clarity?
2. Do you start the day with intent, eager and excited to face the challenges that lie ahead?
3. Do you believe in your potential and the value of your contribution and the value you add to your clients' lives?
4. Do you know that you have something unique to offer your clients and are open to discover new ways to continue adding value to your client's lives?

5. Do you take the time to be reflective about your life path and practice and how you are developing as a practitioner?

Next time you feel inspired by a new idea or perhaps a fresh role model in your life, somebody you meet by chance, or you have a certain gut feeling that won't go away, embrace these new feelings well and use the experience to its full advantage. Nothing happens by chance; everything in life happens for a reason, so don't allow yourself to procrastinate and simply exist. Seek out the inspiration and motivation you need to lead a full and exciting life as a practitioner, follow your star, live your dream and see where it takes you.

• Motivational Questioning Skills

We've looked at the importance of building rapport, mirroring and matching, pacing and leading your client, we're now going to look at a different set of skills you need to feel confident with to secure the ongoing trust and respect of your client. The key skills are:

- Open questioning
- Reflective Listening
- Asking Permission
- Giving feedback
- Generalising statements
- Reversal quantifiers
- Linkage quantifiers
- Using your voice

• Why you should use Open Questions

The use of open questions is vital, as you are looking for your client to open up and give you factual, relevant and sometimes very personal information.

Almost everyone knows that the basic rule is to avoid asking a question to which the response can be yes or no. Anyone with children quickly learns this skill. What we're going to add is what Mark calls "360 degree open questioning".

This is a style of questioning in which each question is formed around one of the following words (or often all of them in the same question if appropriate):

- More
- Better
- Different
- Less

If you use your 360 degree question as a starting point it is guaranteed to open up the client and lead onto deeper discussions and questions. So, for example:

"With your blood sugar imbalance in mind what do you feel you could do more of or better to get it under better control?" Or

"With your weight loss and fitness goals in mind what do you feel you could do less of or differently to see faster, more sustained results?"

• Reflective Listening

It has often been said that the split between client and therapist in a verbal interaction is – ideally - an 80/20 split, with 80% being credited to the client. Obviously if the client is, potentially, speaking 80% of the time, you need to develop your listening skills!

Sounds obvious and easy. We all know how to listen, after all. Well, it's not so easy. Some practitioners really struggle with this as they are natural talkers and leaders; they'll listen to the basic facts, but they prefer to be telling the client what they should do and how they should do it. Then there's the afternoon drift problem, when after a succession of clients we can suddenly find ourselves thinking about how many sessions we have left, and when we're going to eat, and will we have time to get to the shops...

So you need to work at Reflective listening. This focuses around allowing the client to speak as a priority while you pay complete attention - which should be reflected in your, body language, even down to your posture and eye movements. It's a way of building empathy and understanding.

The trick to Reflective listening and to keep your focus and attention is to give yourself an active job to do. If you've ever seen Simon interviewing someone you'd soon become aware that a bomb could go off and he would still be listening. That's because as a journalist his job doesn't end when the interviewee stops talking; that's when it starts: he's got to reproduce accurately what they said. That's your job as a Reflective, active listener. While you are listening to your client, have it in mind that at frequent intervals you are going to summarise what they are saying and reflect it back to them, to check with them that you've understood. To do this you have to stay alert.

For example:

"So, let me just check - what you're saying is that you really want to cut down on your drinking, but you're under pressure to socialise at work. So you're drinking wine at lunchtimes every day and sometimes spirits in the evenings – is that right?"

"If I've understood what you're saying, you feel you're done with stage one of the diet plan, you've got all the new foods sorted and you're ready to move to stage 2. If that's right, let's get straight on with that."

• Asking Permission

It is professional and courteous when asking clients for information to ask permission first. You have a much better chance of getting the information you need if you show them courtesy and respect. You are also reinforcing on an unconscious level that your client is in control of proceedings. For example:

- With you permission, can we talk about..?
- If you don't mind, could we discuss...?
- With your agreement can we talk about...?
- If you are comfortable to talk about ....perhaps we can look at that now?

• Giving Feedback

Again, the greatest leverage you have with giving feedback is always asking permission first. Nobody likes to be told, so you would simply ask your client for permission to give them some feedback on the matter in question. Once you have given the feedback, always thank the client for taking the feedback from you. Feedback should always be positioned as external input and "just a suggestion" about ways of improving and doing things better.

• Generalising Statements

As with our suggestions for your active role in Reflective listening, Generalizing statements are used to summarise a client's particular circumstances. The difference is that you are summarizing the whole case in a single statement.

This not only confirms your understanding to your client but also allows you to immediately move on to potential suggestions. It is another opportunity for them to correct you if you've missed something, or misunderstood.

• Reversal Quantifiers

It's human nature to always want what we can't have. Reversal quantifiers are a style of questioning that embraces an element of reverse psychology with a view to motivating the client into action.

Similarly, you can use reversal quantifiers to challenge clients indirectly to force the appropriate change. For example:

"Thanks for explaining that, Gemma. It seems to me from listening that you may not be quite ready or strong enough to make the change required at this stage..."

• Linkage Quantifiers

Linkage quantifiers are questions which sole aim are to keep the client talking, especially when discussing areas of great sensitivity or upset and you don't want to interrupt the flow.

The art is to simply repeat the client's last word or two - normally given to you at the clients peak state, (peak state statements, as they are sometimes referred to) to keep the client interacting with you verbally and avoid drying up!

Client:	I feel so upset and betrayed I can't continue
Practitioner:	Upset and betrayed?
Client:	Yes, so betrayed I will never be able to trust him again.
Practitioner:	Never trust him again?
Client:	No, never be able to believe a single word he says. I can't believe he would do that, especially with the neighbour!
Practitioner:	The neighbour?
Client:	Yes, the neighbour, didn't I mention it was the neighbour he has been seeing all this time? I tell you I am going to...

Sorry, we have to leave it there. You'll have to tune into our second edition to find out what happened. No but seriously, you can at once see how effective this can be and also how insanely irritating it can get if you overdo it. Sales people are taught this technique and it is awful when misused, so use sparingly.

• Using your Voice

The tone of your voice plays a great part in both keeping rapport and in pacing and leading your client. There are three basic levels of voice tonality and this is how each level works.

Level 1 High pitch

When you raise the tone of your voice, your client's unconscious mind will process it as if you are asking a question. Think about it for a moment, then go into the next room and ask someone a question. You will notice immediately your voice has gone up, especially at the end of your statement. Again, don't overuse this with clients – it can become a hard habit to break. There's a version of this aptly dubbed the "moronic interrogative", which seems to have spread from California and Australia, in which people raise the tone at the end of everything? So they turn everything into a question? I'm sure you've heard it?

Level 2 Level pitch

This tone we know as level tone and is used in normal everyday interaction and communication; it speaks with someone's conscious mind.

Level 3 Low pitch

This is the tone of influence. As we drop our tone down we are communicating directly with our client's unconscious mind.

Remember, the conscious mind deals with a maximum of five or so things at one time; it is normally tied up processing your decisions and thoughts on a moment by moment basis throughout the day.

The unconscious mind processes and stores millions of bits of information. This consists of every past experience and event. This is the place where our values and beliefs are housed. The unconscious mind is often referred to as the computer centre of the mind, where each file represents a real life past event, experience, association, and emotion.

When communicating directly with our client's unconscious mind we can help our clients go where they need to go, by using direct or indirect subliminal suggestions. When dropping the voice down we also find our voice will have a relaxing affect with our clients and often assist in the overall quality of the session.

• Motivational Interviewing - Top Techniques

Motivated clients believe more in what they are doing and take more action, which increases their levels of confidence and commitment, which always leads to greater results, which increase motivation.

Motivation = Belief = Action = Confidence = Results = Increased Motivation... it's simply a cycle which if you get right just keeps on fuelling the client's motivation to take more action. Now you know the questioning skills you need, we can move on to lay out how to use these as part of a complete Motivational Interviewing system. These are the 8 areas we'll be looking at:

1. Is the client is ready for their desired change and if not, where they are on the "ready to change" scale, using the STEAR model
2. Client Contracting - gaining client buy-in and commitment

3. Client Goals and Actions -Investigate goals applying the SMART principles
4. Client compliance -assess the client's ability to follow through on agreed actions and goals using GROW coaching model
5. Identifying client's core beliefs and values
6. Motivate and inspire the client into achieving the results they desire
7. Empowering the client -inside and outside of the therapy room
8. Client's body language -giving a true reflection of how the client's really feeling at any given point

• 50% Fail: how STEAR can help

With programmes that involve three sessions or more, it's fairly typical that 50% of clients fail to see it through to the end. This causes frustration for the practitioner and disappointment for the client, who may then turn into one of those people who says, "Oh yeah, I tried CAM and it didn't work".

There are a number of key factors which help stop this happening.

1. Recognising if the client is ready for the change they desire and where they are on the scale of being ready to make the change.
2. Using change-eliciting questions to get the client to talk about their current situation, why they want to change and what the change will mean to them in the future.
3. I often use a scale of discomfort to measure whether a client is ready for change or not. "Using a scale of 1 to 10 where the nearer to ten you rate yourself the more ready you are to make your desired change, how would you rate yourself right now?"

4. The use of the Life Practice model STEAR© to complete some self-analysis and diagnostics with the client

The STEAR© model provides a structure for a series of questions you ask that will help you judge how ready to change your client is. Having this information is vital as it helps you help them to set achievable goals – you will need to scale them down if they rate low - understand the client and let you know whether there is more work to be done to get them to where they need to be to make the appropriate change. When you know where they are you will be able to pace and lead the client appropriately.

STEAR stands for: **S**ituation, **T**ask, **E**xpectation, **R**esults, **T**ask. Using STEAR© questions you ask them to rate themselves on a scale of 1 to 10 with 10 being completely ready for change and 1 being not ready, over the five areas.

Situation

What is your client's current situation? Get an accurate, as near-objective assessment as possible. Can they continue in this way?

Task

Is your client aware of the changes that need to be made to achieve the results they desire?

Expectation

We can often use SMART again here. Are the client's expectations of change specific, realistic and achievable, and is there a timescales involved.

Action

Does your client understand the levels of action required to make the appropriate change and if so are they able to step up?

Results

Has your client visualised what the impact of these changes will mean, not just on themselves, but on family, friends, work colleagues and so on, and are they ready to cope with the outcome of the action they will be taking?

Using a set of open and relevant questions will help you reach a decision, and if you combine these questions with the scale of discomfort you will have a good idea of where the client sits on the "ready to change scale".

Scoring Indicators

1. Up to 15 = Not ready for change
2. 15 - 25= Ready to begin considering change
3. 25 - 35= Ready to begin to change
4. 35+= Ready for change

You can develop the conversation further by using clever open questions; after all, the more information you have on your client's readiness to change the more effective you will be in helping them achieve that change – and sustaining it. Here are some suggestions:

Situation

- What would you like to be different about your current situation?
- Currently what makes you feel the most need to change?
- What will happen if you don't make any change now?

- What will be the immediate benefits to you of making this change?
- How ready do you feel to make the changes you want to make?
  On a scale of 1 to 10, 10 representing complete readiness to change and 1 meaning not ready for change on any level where would you put yourself right now?

Task

- What resources do you have that will help you make the changes you desire right now?
- What action have you taken recently to begin making three lifestyle changes you've decided to make?
- What goals and actions would help you with your planned changes?
- What is the downside, if any, of making this change?

Expectation

- Looking ahead, how do you see your life once you have made the change?
- What's the best thing that can happen from you making these changes?
- What's the worst thing that can happen if you make these changes?
- Where will you be in ten years' time if you don't make these changes?
- What are you expecting to enjoy once you have made these changes?

Action

- What action have you taken up to now to do things differently?

- How much time are you allowing for your actions to make this desired change this week?
- What are you prepared to do to ensure you succeed with your plans?
- What are you prepared to do right now, today, to begin your programme?

Results

- What will be the impact on the people around you when you make these changes?
- How will you deal with the results this change will bring to your life?
- What will be the impact of making these changes on your job and your daily routine?
- How important is this change to you?

• Use Past, Present and Future Questioning

PPF questioning is used when asking the client to visualise the past, present and future in relation to making the appropriate change or not. It can be very powerful and make it that extra real to the client. Examples:

- If you think of a big change you made in the past, think for a moment, what would have happened if you hadn't made that change?
- Think about certain situations that you find yourself in today and think - what would be different now if you had taken action and made that change earlier?
- Think into the future and ask yourself how the change you are contemplating making now will impact on your future success. How will it be?

• **Sensory Questioning**

The NLP model teaches us we all process information differently. We process information using our senses, our representational systems, and we all prefer to use one or a combination, over the others.

VAKOG reminds us that our main senses are Visual - Auditory - Kinesthetic -Olfactory – Gustatory. Eyes, ears, mouth, nose, feel and taste. It also helps us to know that most human beings are VK - Visual and Kinesthetic.

If we know how our client prefers to process information we can communicate with them more effectively. Given that most of us emphasise what we feel and what we see helps us to choose our language carefully. It means we can start by using words like "see" and "feel" a lot. For example:

- What do you see when making this change to your life?
- How do you feel this change will benefit your life in the future?
- What do you see and feel when we discuss making these changes to your life?
- What would you like to see different about your current situation?
- Why do you feel the need to change?

All this helps us get to an understanding of where our clients are on their journey of change. If you let STEAR© give the structure to your open questions you will now be in a position to begin successful change work with your client, knowing you have just increased the chances for full compliance and follow through on agreed goals and actions.

To get consistent top results there are two more strategies you need: contracting and timing.

• Client Contracting

A contract can be a legal binding document or simply a verbal agreement between two people. Some of you who graduated from one of the more informed training courses may have been introduced to Learning Contracts. In the clinic context what we're talking about is a kind of Service Level Agreement – but one that your client signs on to as well.

With a contract agreed and signed both client and practitioner know what to expect of each other and what are the parameters of the relationship. This is also the place to agree on a frequency of sessions; you need to see your client regularly to build momentum. You can always cut back the frequency as things progress.

When working with demotivated clients, using a form of agreement from the outset helps gee them up to follow through on agreed actions.

The contract

You don't need anything too formal - after all you don't want to frighten the client away! However getting your written obligations to one another is a must, whether it be on a standard client session notes form or on a form designed for purpose. The contract should include:

- The name of both practitioner and client
- Current date
- Duration of sessions
- Individual responsibilities
- Client actions
- Practitioner actions
- Frequency of sessions
- Client goals and plans
- Current progress
- Goal review

Both client and practitioner hold a copy of the contract and as progress is made it is updated with current progress and achievements. This can prove to be very motivational for the client and inspires them to take their actions and goals seriously and follow through on what they have agreed.

It is important to get an agreement on the frequency of sessions. Decide with the client how many sessions you believe you need to deliver the required results, and what the time gap should be between sessions.

• Client Contact Strategy: when do you see them again?

This addresses a debate that has been doing the rounds for some years now across all CAM disciplines but probably most of all with nutritional therapists.

Mark was recently involved in a coaching session with a large group of highly experienced nutritional therapists. They were struggling, business was slow and they needed an injection of new ideas. Their standard procedure was that following an initial lengthy consultation, they would not see a client for the second client appointment until 6 weeks later. When Mark asked how many clients turned up for that second consultation, he wasn't too surprised to learn it was 39%.

Practitioners all over the UK are failing because they don't get this bit right. And you'll find plenty of people who'll disagree vehemently with us on the "frequency" issue. Just ask them for their figures.

In the shoes of our client

Let's think about our potential client once more. We've established that it may have taken her six months to pluck up the courage to look for a practitioner and finally make an appointment. After all that, she gets to see you, gets inspired – and then is told you don't want to see her again for six weeks. Well I know how I would feel and what I would do.

The proven model

When working with any client you need to really get close, understand that client's issues and build momentum for change. You cannot do that with a six-week gap. Begin with weekly sessions, moving to fortnightly and monthly as progress is made.

This way you can continually motivate and inspire your client. This is a model that we know works. Weekly face to face contact facilitates the success of the sessions and gives better and more sustainable results. This has been proved many times over in successful coaching models from all over the world.

The dynamics of a successful client relationship and contact strategy and born out of trust and a strong foundation of rapport. Whenever I am agreeing with the client how often sessions should be held, weekly is always the first answer. They feel comfortable. Yes, it can vary from therapy to therapy and practitioner to practitioner, but have a close look at what happens if you opt for long time gaps between sessions.

Have the confidence to change

Just because it may always have been this way in your particular field that doesn't mean it has to stay that way. You may have even been trained in a certain way, with a certain process. Still, don't be afraid to try new things.

• Client Goals and Actions

An idea is just an idea until you write it down. A goal is just a dream until you write it down and take action.

With your skills you can bring a client's goals alive with them, turning them from dreams into reality, by getting them written down, forming a strategy and developing a plan to achieve them.

There are many things you could discuss at the beginning of your first session and this may be a new concept to some of you, but bear in mind that this is part of the opening strategy of highly successful practitioners like Michael Ash and Anthony Haynes – and one of the key processes they teach in their Profitable Practice seminars – and is also part of the NLP and coaching model adopted in the nutritional therapy degree course at the CNELM (see our interview with Kate Neil in chapter 6).

Think of it like this. We all enjoy talking about ourselves and our dreams and goals in life, so bringing this up front to the beginning of your client meeting is easy to do and will set the tone for the rest of your sessions. You client will see you are taking action with them from your first moments together, which will both motivate them and gain you credibility.

Going one step farther, you should begin every session with a review of their goals. Celebrate successes achieved together! This is very motivational.

• Setting goals

1 Ensure goals are CSMART

Client Commitment , **S**pecific, **M**easurable, **R**ealistic and have **T**imescales. CSMART is an integral part of the goal-setting process as it goes right to the heart of the structure and realism of goals. It's obviously counter-productive to set unrealistic, unachievable goals or goals that are too big a stretch in too short a time. That leads to struggle and you will probably lose the client.

Apply CSMART to every individual goal and make sure every goal meets the criteria.For example:

"I want to lose loads of weight and feel good as soon as possible so I look good in Spain on my holiday in my bikini" is not CSMART.

"My goal is to work out 3 times per week and stop eating chocolate in order for me to lose two pounds per week between now and when I go on holiday in July of this year" is CSMART: it demonstrates client commitment, is specific and realistic.

2 Only work with a maximum of 5 goals

A common mistake practitioners make is to set lots of goals with their clients. Prioritise! Pick the most important five goals and start with those. That way you keep things simple and focused. Too many goals will dilute their importance and end up confusing or overwhelming your client.

3 Recognise high-impact goals

Sometimes when a client has an obvious important priority, the first step will be to establish a handful (normally 3) of high-impact goals and actions to address that specific problem or situation. High impact goals, deliver high impact actions, which deliver priority results fast.

4 Set short, medium and long term goals

If you are going to do the job properly the client should be working with a set of short (6 months), medium (18 months) and long term (2 years) goals. 70 % of effort and action should go into short term goals, 20% into medium and 10% into longer term goals. Clients typically end up with 3 or so short term goals, 1 medium and 1 long term.

5 Client actions

Once you have agreed the goals (the "what" in the client's strategy), you now have to agree the "how", which takes the form of client actions.

It is sensible to apply CSMART here also to ensure actions are realistic and achievable. Also set up times to review progress together. This again can be very motivational and inspirational for the client when they see themselves making progress

5 Own a "practitioner action"

It's easy to allow the client to own all the actions. Let them do all the work, right? Many practitioners feel this is right; however you can obtain excellent results by owning and taking away a minimum of 1 action that you agree to do to support your client. This inspires and motivates your client even more, as they really feel you are working together. It doesn't have to be anything huge – it can be agreeing to do some research for them, to source a supplement or remedy, or to give them a check-up call between sessions.

6 Acknowledge and celebrate progress

Your client now has a strategy, a set of goals and actions that are moving them towards better health and a more fulfilling life. How they feel as they move through this process is fundamental to whether they stick with the programme or not

Your mission – and you SHOULD choose to accept it – is to continue to inspire and motivate them throughout this entire process. A powerful and essential step in this is for you to notice, acknowledge and celebrate progress.Even if they are somewhat off the pace from where you had hoped they would, ANY sign of progress and accomplishment needs celebrating and rewarding.

Use ANY sign of improvement as leverage to prove to the client they can do it. As soon as they start to see regular results, however small, they will build their own momentum. The more results they see, the more momentum they will build.

Mark's Modelling Tip

It is motivational and inspirational for the client to bring goal-setting to the forefront of your agenda. Spend a large chunk of the first session discussing the client's goals.

• Now review: the GROW model

GROW is used all over the world in business, commerce, and both private and public sector staff personal development; it can be found almost everywhere where a review of performance is required; it is now regularly used throughout the CAM industry where supervision is applied.

Whenever we are working with clients we need a process to review a client's goals and actions and GROW fits the bill. Use it at any given agreed review point, which can be weekly, fortnightly, monthly, even annually.

GROW stands for **G**oal, **R**eality, **O**ptions, **W**ay forward.

Goal

The client's goal.

Reality

Current reality at the point of review: where is the client in relation to their goals and what is the reality of the client achieving them?

Options

What are the client's options at this stage? Do we need to review the goal, agree new actions, implement new strategies?

Way forward

Future actions and plans agreed by you both.

Top Tips for using GROW

- Ensure the information you are reviewing is up to date and accurate.
- Ensure the results achieved to date are correct and agreed by the practitioner and client.
- Praise the client where it is evident improvement has been made.
- Equally important: question the client where it is clear progress hasn't been made.
- Ensure revised future actions are agreed in full with the client.
- Ensure you have full client buy-in at all times in the process.
- When planning revised/future goals follow the CSMART principle.
- Document any changes to the plan and update the client goals and action plan accordingly.
- Don't lose sight of the fact GROW is simply a coaching strategy:the client's results, levels of buy-in and motivation and ultimately results, always come first
- The GROW model is a tool to assist both you and the client in reviewing client progress. It can be a fractious time, especially if no progress is being made, so be prepared to find things to praise and use all of your inspirational and motivational skills to keep the client motivated.
- Always document the GROW review and discussions on your client session notes form and ensure the client leaves with a copy of the notes so they are clear on agreed future actions.

• Client Compliance

Client compliance reflects their "readiness for change". It also reflects how skillfully you conduct your consultation.

CAM Award winner for Outstanding Practice Antony Haynes is acknowledged as one of the UK's most successful practitioners, and he famously told Simon in a CAM magazine interview: "Practitioners often used to ask me, 'How'd you get people to do that?' And I'd say, 'Well, how come you don't? You mean your patients don't do what you ask? I don't understand.' So then I had two of my colleagues sit in with me and take notes about what happened in the consultations and now we teach this as part of the 'Profitable Practice' course."

When his colleagues modelled Antony it turned out that there were 32 different things he was doing in a consultation, most of them in a specific sequence. It's that attention to detail, to covering the bases, that will have a big impact on how willing your client is to stay the course.

We've already seen that with programmes that involve three sessions or more, over 50% of clients fail to see the programme through. There's more bad news:

- 26% of clients don't turn up for their first appointment
- 44% of clients fail to make it through to their 2nd appointment
- 50% fail to make it through to their 3rd appointment
- More than 75% of people fail to complete a programme of six sessions or more

Now supposing you're including goal-setting and agreed actions. These are some figures that have emerged:

- 80% of clients are late when returning paperwork to a practitioner
- 61% of clients don't return the paperwork at all
- More than 50% of clients don't follow through on agreed actions

- When working a structured programme with a practitioner, more than 50% of clients drop out prematurely
- When agreeing goals with a practitioner 75% of clients don't write them down
- Only 10% of people actually achieve their goals

One of the hardest challenges we face as practitioners is to get a client to follow through on their goals and agreed actions. As you can see, this is even after they have set these goals with a practitioner and seem to understand all the benefits adhering to these goals will mean to them. Unfortunately this seems to be the default state for humans.

Take New Year's Resolutions.Every year it's thought that 90% of people all over the world set new goals, have new ideas, and believe they are going to change their lives for the better in the New Year ahead. By December 31 between 10 and 20% of people have actually achieved what they set out to achieve. That's 1 in 5 to 1 in 10, depending on whose research you look at. That's how good we are at following through as human beings.

Psychologists from Freud onwards have acknowledged that as humans, our nature is to always follow the path of least resistance.

So that's bad news, right? Well, not really. First, as Antony and his colleague Michael Ash have proved, non-compliance is not inevitable. Second, as this is embedded in human nature, it's not ALL your fault.

Feel better?

Let's start looking at some solutions.

1. Categorise your clients

The first step is to understand there are different types of client you are going to be working with and that you do have a choice about whom you take on as a client.

A lot of clients won't be ready for the change they think they might need or want (if in doubt apply STEAR©). These may be clients who are coming to see you because someone else wants them to, for example. There are others you realise you just can't help; as Rebecca Smith told us in chapter 6: "You can't help everyone, so don't be afraid to refer a client on."

Once you have understood and accepted this break your clients down into six different categories.

1. The client who's not ready to change
2. The client who doesn't want to change but someone else wants them to (typically been sent by spouse)
3. The procrastinating client who wants to change but keeps putting it off
4. The client who wants to change but lacks the confidence and self-belief to do so
5. The client who wants and needs to see you as their problem makes getting effective help a priority
6. The client who thinks they can't afford you

We are in the business of facilitating change in our clients; we're not waving a magic wand and having miracles happen. Every client has the ability to change and get at least partway towards their desired state of health; we're just there to help. With that in mind, if we take an honest look at the six categories, it's clear we don't want to be working with categories 1 or 2, possibly even number 3 – unless we like a challenge - so that leaves us with 4, 5 and 6.

As we learned earlier we would apply STEAR© to analyse the readiness for change certainly with 4 and 6, and that will help you work out exactly how to approach their treatment.

Mark's Modelling Tip

Never take on a client who isn't ready or doesn't want to change. Often you find someone sitting in front of you who really doesn't want to be there, but a member of their family has pushed them into coming to see you. Explain politely they are wasting their money, and send them home.

2. Ask your client to email you a timeline of their problem

You can tell a lot from a written piece of work and you will also be able to apply STEAR© to their words and have a good idea where they are on the change scale. This way you learn a lot about your client and their perception of themselves.

You also get to see how compliant and enthusiastic they are by seeing if they send you the timeline by the date you asked for it.

3. Insist on an initial consultation before starting formal sessions

An initial consultation is generally free; the sole purpose is to give both you and the client an opportunity to check each other out. You can meet face to face or do this on the phone.

This is the ideal time for you both to be transparent about what you expect and need from each other to ensure the relationship works. Following through on agreed actions is something to raise here, and make it clear what you expect once actions and goals have been agreed.

Position this up front and explain it is for the benefit of the client as he or she will need to be completely committed if you are going to get results.

4. The contract method

We've already touched on this. It's used very successfully by many practitioners and improves follow-through rates incredibly.

You must never lose site of the fact we are talking about a paying client here and they needed to be treated with your utmost respect. When you use your great rapport-building skills combined with exuding professionalism as you explain the need for this kind of agreement, most clients accept the idea.

Many successful practitioners find it works extremely well to write up the client's goals and actions for them. It can add weight to the relationship.

5. Client Goals and GROW

We looked in depth earlier at the importance of goals and actions. If you make sure you always have a good plan, a realistic set of goals and achievable actions all under the umbrella of being managed through the GROW model, you won't go far wrong.

Always deliver on what you promise and take at least one action away yourself to do for the client so they can see you really are working together on achieving their goals.

Mark's Modelling Tip

When working with clients and reviewing their achievement through the GROW model a great golden rule is "Watch what they do, not what they say".

This will enable you to focus on the objective results and actions of your client and you'll recognise when your client may be making excuses or only giving you half the truth.

• Client Body Language

Do you ever wonder what your client is really trying to tell you? Are they telling the truth or is there some hidden message or meaning that you're missing or don't understand? How do you get to the bottom of what they are really thinking?

Understanding your client's body language is vital when trying to find out what your client really wants, really feels, and most importantly what they are trying to really tell you.

When Richard Bandler and Dr John Grinder were investigating the art and science of human behaviour and developing NLP back in the 1970s, several lessons were learned. They weren't the first to discover, but they were certainly the first to make such a big deal out of it, that we don't just communicate by talking to each other's conscious minds. Bandler and Grinder suggested that we communicate far more unconsciously than we had ever realised.

One of the key facts to come out of the research was that it is quite common for the human mind to be thinking about one thing consciously and maybe talking about it quite convincingly, while at the same time "unconsciously" giving out very different communication signals. The classic example of this is when you see someone in conversation saying to their partner "I totally agree with you!" while shaking their head and crossing their arms.

If a client does that you, then the message is obvious. Well, obvious-ish. Maybe they think what you are saying is rubbish. On the other hand, they may think you're a genius, but inside they're feeling really scared about what you're suggesting they do. So...don't jump to any conclusions, but the mismatch surely signals that there's something going on that you need to find out about.

Here are some basics which will help you read what your client is "really" saying, or telling you unconsciously without realising it. But remember to always investigate. These are generalisations and may not be true for everyone you find in front of you.

1. Look into my eyes

- Blinking – increased blinking correlates with heightened anxiety or attentiveness.
- Controlled blinking, even if only milliseconds slower than spontaneous blinking, together with longer closure, is often associated with deception.
- Pupil dilation – eyes enlarge when light dims but also when someone is excited, aroused, happy or engaged in problem- solving activities.
- Sporadic eye contact suggests a lack of confidence; generally accompanied by lots of shuffling and looking away (but again remember, a minority of people just prefer not to look you in the eye so that they can better focus on hearing what you are saying.

2. What's on their face?

Your client may be talking positively, but what is their facial expression saying? Our faces disclose a range of feelings, from anger to sadness, disappointment to elation, jubilation to surprise and so on.

3. Is your client listening to you?

- Lowering the body, averting eyes and moving away are non-verbal clues that signal submissiveness.
- Pointing feet towards you may indicate positive feelings about you. If the feet are pointed away from you while the body faces you, that is a sign of discomfort.

- Playing with the nose is a definite indication they are miles away
- Wrapping a foot behind a leg during a conversation is a defensive posture and can suggest they are worried by what you are saying.

4 Does your client feel comfortable with you?

- When you find a client leaning away from you, or looking up at you from the chair, that can suggest they are uncomfortable in the situation or with the conversation.
- Others of the same to watch out for are hand over the mouth, crossing of the legs or arms, dry mouth or slightly more obvious signs in underarm or facial sweats. Your client in these cases is definitely not comfortable with what you are saying or doing.

5. Has your client had enough?

- An old favourite of Mark's is when a client appears to be listening to you intently, but has a hand placed on one of their face cheeks or a finger on one of the temples, which immediately suggests there is an awful lot of inner dialogue going on and they are probably not listening to you at all!
- Continual touching of the watch or movement of the watch face or strap definitely confirms your client wants to be as far away as possible, probably hasn't taken in a single word over the last few minutes and can't wait to leave.
- Racing through the paperwork you have just given them to read and focusing on the back page within seconds of it being given out indicates they are working out when they will be free to leave and go and do something else.

• **Empower your Client**

Empowering your client in the time they spend with you is important. Empowering your client to be totally free and teaching them life-changing strategies they can use in the time they are away from you (in between sessions) and liberating your client for ever, is the Holy Grail of all motivational and inspirational activity.

As CAM practitioners our mission includes educating our clients about their health, about nutrition and lifestyle practices that will maintain their wellbeing for years to come.

What does it mean to empower?

- Having the skills to be able teach your clients strategies that give them a greater sense of well-being and confidence.
- Equipping your clients with the tools, skills and knowledge to enable them to go on to achieve their life's dreams, goals and ambitions without you.
- Enabling others to reach the highest levels of health and vitality that are possible for them to reach. Along with this may go personal and professional development.

The dynamics of the relationship have to be right to be able to empower your client. The client will need to:

- Respect you
- Trust you
- Believe you
- Be committed to change

You as a practitioner will need to:

- Educate the client
- Set realistic goals

- Follow a structured programme
- Set the client tasks outside of the sessions
- Teach the client strategies for eating, shopping, relaxation, exercise etc that they can do in their own time
- Ensure regular updates and follow-through
- Work with the client to explore strategies and options
- Provide recommended reading and projects for clients to do in their own time
- Encourage the client to take responsibility for their own results and give them daily tasks to complete, even if it's just reading something you recommend
- Teach the client the techniques they normally do with you in sessions – for example EFT (Emotional Freedom Technique) or Tapping as it's widely known. Why make the client wait until the next session with you when they can be taking action every day on their own.

All of the above help the client use their own time productively away from the sessions with you. It helps the client find a multitude of different ways to help them work through the change cycle themselves, so eventually you become just one of a number of strategies the client is using to meet their goals.

The weighting of this relationship changes towards fewer sessions and more client activity, until eventually the client works successfully on their own, maybe coming to you for periodic check-ups and testing.

Chapter 9: Managing your own Stress

Working in this field opens us up continually to other people's issues and stress - after all that's what we are here for. However as practitioners we need to keep a very close eye on our own stress levels.

Some of the best practitioners in the world light a candle in between each session to clear the room of any negative energy, or mentally surround themselves with a ball of white light to protect them from the stress of their clients. There are many things we can do and here we've focused on the more down to earth strategies.

But first, let's hear from ace nutritional therapist Antony Haynes, winner of a CAM Award for Outstanding Practice, who's had first-hand experience of practice-related stress. Talking to Simon in an interview for CAM, he said:

"I learned a long, long time ago that if I started a clinic day in a flustered state, very much involved with my "stuff", that it was a struggle for the day. The more I let in whatever was going on in my life, or what was going on in the world in general, then the more of struggle it was and I ended up with a headache at the end of every single clinic day.

"I was drinking water and eating well, and I was thinking, 'What's going on?' I basically realised that I simply couldn't carry on doing it.

I love the one-to-one process and the realisation, the insights, and the inspiration and motivation that I could confer to people. I love that. But boy, I could only do that with three or four people before I started getting a headache!

"I discovered that I was setting my mind to try to figure out what I was going to say, what I was going to recommend when it came to that stage in the consultation. So part of my brain was trying to find all those mental 'files' with all the information that I was going to need to be able to come up with a plan, and I wasn't 100% in the now. I was actually, dare I say, 15 or 20 minutes in the future, thinking about what I was going to recommend.

"I found that instead, by starting the day with the intention that I would be the very best practitioner for that patient, meaning that I would be 100% in the now for them, means I can now go 12 hours straight through... without any problem with energy or headaches whatsoever. I take no phone calls, no texts, no emails, absolutely nothing.

"What I'm aiming for is complete and utter devotion and dedication to the patient in front of me at the moment in time. The only time is now. There is no stress in that time. So before I meet someone, I imagine them, that I'm going to be the best practitioner for them, and of course, that means setting aside time for listening and to appreciate where they're at. And you can't fake it."

Antony has a second technique that he says produces not just a stress-free work experience, but makes it effortless.

"The juxtaposition is very interesting", he says. "One is an intention or attitude, and the other one is absolutely focusing on the practical detail of the process of the consultation.

"Because I find the process, if it's done appropriately, becomes an effortless process where power is generated. I call it 'power' in the sense of it being a very powerful experience. And that's the feeling the patient will get. It's something I've worked very hard at. And then, because I got the feedback that a lot of people weren't having that experience with their patients, I then analysed it, and now I can appreciate why that happens.

"So there is a process by which to inspire or motivate, and it's a process, once set up, which requires writing out the bullet points for the consultation on the page, and requires a discipline to conduct the consultation in that sequence and to make sure you've covered as many of the 32 things as possible. And some of those are very, very small. They just take a second. Some take more than a few seconds.

"It's a process. I find the detail in the process makes it effortless, and the patient feels that they're the centre of the universe, and they are in that time – they're the complete focus."

(Antony Haynes, BA (Hons), Dip ION, mBANT, is Head of Technical Services and cofounder of Nutri-Link. With colleague Michael Ash he runs "Profitable Practice" seminars: www. nleducation.co.uk)

Here are our top 6 strategies.

• Get Your Own Mentor

Most of the highly successful practitioners, coaches and businesspeople in the world have their own coaches or mentors. This I something that is lacking in the CAM field so far – and an idea we'd like to see take hold.

With legislation going the way it is, practitioners will soon be required to have a formal professional supervision scheme in place. Mentors and coaches can take this on.

If it's true that 85%-90% of practitioners go into January each year determined to make some positive change for themselves and their practice in the following 12 months and only 12% actually achieve what they set out to do, these figures are reversed when a mentor is deployed.

Private mentoring is becoming more available and more affordable.

What is mentoring?

"Mentoring is to support and encourage people to manage their own learning in order that they may maximise their potential, develop their skills, improve their performance and become the person they want to be." - Eric Parsloe, the Oxford School of Coaching & Mentoring: www.oscm. co.uk

It's quite common for practitioners to informally mentor and coach each other. Whereas this does serve the purpose of letting go of any daily frustrations or challenges, a professional mentor will help take you and your practice to another level.

What's the difference between coaching and mentoring?

A mentoring relationship can often last for a long time with no fixed period while coaching tends to have a set duration. Mentoring is less formal and meetings and interaction tends to follow the needs of the client, with face to face or telephone chats, as well as spontaneous email and text conversations. Coaching is (usually) far more structured, with meetings set on a regular basis.

Mentoring tends to focus on the development of the mentee as a person, where coaching usually addresses the development of a skill or a set of actions

What's in it for you?

- Being able to change/achieve your goals more quickly and effectively than working alone
- Building a network of expertise to draw on that can benefit both yourself and others

- Drawing on the skills and knowledge of an expert in your field of expertise
- Modelling the success of your mentor using proven success strategies and ideas that work
- Feeling you are part of a team with an expert team leader working in partnership to assist you with your own personal development needs and goals

How much does it cost?

It is important to establish from day 1 what your needs are as a mentee and make sure your mentor has the time and capabilities to meet your needs. To work, this relationship has to be free of any time constraints, logistical constraints and financial constraints. In addition, trust and rapport are vital ingredients in any relationship and are no different in this one. It is normal to find a good mentor with unlimited contact and support from around £200 per month.

Meanwhile – team up

If affordability is an issue – and of course it will be when you are first starting out, then two heads are better than one. At the very least team up with another like-minded practitioner so you have a regular outlet for your stress.

Meet at least weekly for a minimum of a couple of hours as you will find you have issues in common and just talking them through will help. If you have any problem cases that you are unsure about dealing with, talk them through and then see if you need to kick them up for advice from a tutor or more experienced practitioner. If you are a nutritional therapist, then phoning a supplement supplier's Technical Support team may also provide some useful ideas – but don't use them on a regular basis to offload your stress.

Stress is really just feeling overwhelmed and out of control. Being able to share your professional stress, obviously within the bounds of client confidentiality, is a very positive step and one that will help you immensely.

• Model Week

This is a time management strategy and although at first may seem basic, it has been used by some of the most senior business leaders in the UK to help them with long term stress challenges. Thanks to Mark's intervention, many practitioners now adopted Model Week, as it has proved many times to reduce stress while at the same time forcing new and productive behaviors and activities into their everyday working pattern

Let's begin by looking at a selection of stress triggers that practitioners face every day. These were taken from a poll of experienced practitioners:

- Scattered appointments - appointments hours apart
- Inconsistent clinic days
- Picking children up from school
- Personal responsibilities
- Lack of preparation time for clients
- No time to proactively market the practice
- Appointment overload
- Home life
- Lack of private time
- No time to do admin
- CPD
- Lack of appointments

You can probably add many more. Now think about all the things that practitioners do (actually this applies to the entire working population) to justify their time - excluding seeing clients. We can call this time justification. How many times have you thought to yourself, "I've been so busy today", and then realise you haven't actually seen many clients or earned much money. For "time justification" this same group of practitioners came up with:

- Cleared paperwork
- Met interesting people
- Found a good course to go on
- Came up with some good ideas
- Cleaned office or practice
- Filed all my paperwork
- Paid bills
- Answered letters
- Dealt with some advertising salesman
- Enquired about advertising
- Rearranged office
- Spoke to website guy

Again, we know you can add to this list! The point is we are all guilty of feeling like we have put in a hard day's work in our practice - but have we really? Consider this CRAFTI model:

- **Client appointments**
- **Regular breaks**
- **Administration**
- **Family time**
- **Time to go to gym**
- **Income driving activity**

Yes, this CRAFTI anagram of Mark's is kind of ironic. But this is a model of an ideal day that reduces the impact of any long-term stress, as you are including regular breaks and exercise in your daily routine. It also takes care of family and work/home life balance needs. In addition it is driving income and growth into your practice by reserving a slot for income driving activity – every day.

Dedicate 1 hour a day to administration – or Batch Processing (BP) in our Model Week. When the hour is up, focus on your clients and driving your business forward. Administration, however important, does not drive your business and does not make you money. More importantly, it has no impact on the bottom line. All non-income driving paperwork falls into the category of batch processing.

So using CRAFTI to remind us what we need to fit in, and assuming we're seeing 9 clients a week, here's what a Model Week looks like:

Model Week for Practitioners

Time	Monday	Tuesday	Wednesday	Thursday	Friday	Saturday	Sunday
7.30					D	F	F
8.00					A	A	A
9.00	IDA	IDA	IDA	IDA	Y	M	M
10.00	BP	BP		IDA		I	I
11.00	B	B	B	IDA	O	L	L
12.00				B	F	Y	Y
1.00	G	G	G	G	F		
2.00	B	B	B	B			
3.00	CA	CA	CA		R		
4.00	CA	CA	CA	BP	E		
5.00	CA	CA	CA	BP	L		
6.00	F	F	F	F	A		
7.00	F	F	F	F	X		
8.00	F	F	F	F			

BP = Batch Processing, IDA = Income Driving Activity, G = Gym or exercise, F = Family Time, CA = Client appointment, B = break

Personalise this and come up with your own Model Week.

The Big 5 Principles:

1. Effective Time Management to ensure you allow yourself your own time and regular breaks to avoid stress and overload
2. To ensure you dedicate time every day to take the commercial side of your business forward
3. To ensure you have the right balance between work and home life
4. To ensure you are fresh and in a good state of mind to deliver the best results for your clients
5. To ensure you get big on the big things and only dedicate minimum time to non-income driving and non-client facing activity

Mark's Modelling Tip

Begin your day with 1 hour of income driving activity. This could include

- Writing letters to potential client groups
- Proactive marketing
- Following up on enquiries
- Creating future opportunities
- Proactive approaches to joint ventures

Anything that creates income falls into this category of income driving activity. This works and has been proven to work time and time again. Get into the habit of dedicating 1 hour a day every day to driving your business growth forward and you will be successful.

• Use Demands, Constraints and Choices

Do we hear a "Yes, but..."? After working through the Model Week section, you'll have all sorts of everyday tasks and demands running through your mind. So take a pen and paper and write down everything you do in a week

If you have captured everything, you may have up to a hundred tasks listed, maybe even more than that, and you are probably in tears. Sorry. We know, trying to prioritise them into CRAFTI seems impossible. The solution for that is (yet) another very effective model called the Demands, Constraints and Choices model.

(I know, you may be getting "model fatigue" by now. It's Mark's fault. If he hasn't got a model for something he invents one. He's always looking for ones that will fit funny acronyms as well. He failed with this one. But I've had a word. I am fairly certain this is absolutely the LAST model in the book (LMIB) – Simon.)

The sole purpose of this model is to help you look objectively at every one of those tasks listed and put them into one of the following categories:

Demand = A task you have no control over and cannot change. For example, a client's fixed appointment, paying your rent, buying toilet paper. Everything included in CRAFTI is a Demand.

Constraint = A task you have little control over but that does give an element of choice; you may be able to change it in some way. For example, moving a client's appointment, making the last roll of toilet paper last longer.

Choice = A task you have full control over and can freely ignore or put off. Who needs toilet paper?

Once you have completed this exercise you will have 3 columns of tasks. To keep you focused and to manage your time effectively you begin by working the **Demands.** Constraints and Choices would follow subject to the amount of time you have remaining in your Model Week.

Become highly organized and strict with your time. Successful practitioners are ruthless with their time and focus 50% of their time on income driving and client servicing activities

• Develop a Personal Change Plan

One of the greatest stressors we experience as human beings is change. All change. Even change we want to happen. In fact too much change as a cause for human stress is one of the themes running through the successful Human Givens coaching and counselling models. What we know for sure about change is that

1. **Change is coming whether we like it or not.**
2. **We need to accept change and make it work for us not against us.**
3. **Change can be good for business as it creates endless new opportunities and possibilities.**
4. **Resisting change can cause stress and unhappiness.**

Accepting change

This is by far the most productive emotional state to find. We cannot influence Demands (those things that absolutely HAVE to be done), so why waste valuable energy and resources trying?

Find a way of making the change work for you and reframe the change as a positive step, rather than an obstruction.

A good example to use here is regulation. It is already here in some CAM disciplines and it's coming in varying forms of heaviness to others. We cannot resist it. Embrace it. Although it involves extra work and more bureaucracy, we have to assume it has the client's best interests at heart.

See it as a way of getting better at what you do. Reframe it in your own mind as a challenge and one you will enjoy overcoming.

Fear of change

We're afraid of what they don't understand, and often we don't take the time to understand what a change will bring, so we automatically label it as negative. To combat this, it makes sense to have a change plan in place within your business planning and strategy.

Tell yourself you are going to plan to change every 12 months and target yourself on the following:

1. Finding new business opportunities
2. Forming new business relationships every year
3. Creating a further business income stream
4. Keeping up to date with changing client demands

Remember, once you have your plan - write it down. Capture on paper your vision, goals, action plan and strategy, and ensure your plan is SMART. Specific, Measurable, Achievable, Realistic, with Timescales

This will ensure you keep up to date with the changing demands of the market, the needs of your clients and you'll be ahead of the change game.

• Keep up with the latest trends - Tele-Coaching

The needs and demands of our clients are changing all the time and we need to make sure we are "fit for the future" in terms of meeting those new demands.

At the same time the world of information technology is developing at speeds beyond belief. We've already talked about social media and the power of the World Wide Web, but there's one more thing: Tele-Coaching.

Telephone coaching works brilliantly and increases your potential client base to 6 billion overnight. OK, we're exaggerating, but you get the picture. SKYPE is the current vehicle of the day and is excellent for telecoaching clients all over the world, giving you a virtual face-to-face contact from your computer.

Mark's Modelling Tip

Put a direct link to SKYPE on your website under a "Tele-coaching" heading. Change your price and policy page to include international clients (they can use PayPal to send their fees) and away you go.

Of course there are professional constraints. If necessary, instead of offering your Full Monty service, for tele clients you re-position yourself as a Wellbeing Coach. The current economic worries and the dramatic increase in stress levels means many more people are seeking new and different ways to manage and deal with their health concerns. Often they are looking for advice on diet, nutrition and lifestyle choices that to a qualified CAM practitioner seem ridiculously basic. But not everyone is comfortable reading books or researching on the Net – they welcome the guidance of someone who knows the field.

Many Wellbeing Coaches Mark knows and works with saw their practices double in size through 2012.

The latest studies showed the list of wellbeing strategies changing rapidly and already including:

- Face to Face coaching
- Tele Coaching
- Webinars (Live coaching seminars via the internet)
- Computer-based coaching

- Cognitive Behavioural Therapy done directly online
- Podcasts

The must-haves of an effective practitioner-client relationship remain. Trust is vital and respect and rapport have to be there. That said, there is no good reason why every CAM practitioner could not add some form of telephone coaching to the practice.

How long should a telephone coaching session last?

A typical telephone session should last no less than 30 minutes and no more than 60 minutes. This caters for our average attention span. Anything beyond this could become laborious and lose its power and effect. Face to Face sessions tend to take longer than this.

Stress screws with your brain: 5 ways to fight back

Ben Brown

Naturopath Ben Brown, ND, consultant to Nutri Ltd, gives us 5 ways to fight stress and keep our brains in great shape.

Have you ever felt that everything is just all in your head? Well, most of it is. Your brain is the central means by which you interpret your world. Through your brain you are constantly receiving information and then orchestrating how your body responds, every response from a breath to a heartbeat.

Your brain is also your personal lifeguard. When you are exposed to stressful events over which you have no control, events that keep recurring, are irritating, annoying, drain your emotions, exhaust you physically, are dangerous or even life-threatening, it is your brain that keeps your head above water. By producing an adaptive response throughout your body, your brain helps you cope with the pressure. But the short term gain comes at a long term cost.

When stress is prolonged over time your brain starts to melt down, quite literally. Magnetic Resonance Imaging (MRI) studies have found that people under long-term stress have shrinking brains. The same stress response that keeps you going can also be your demise, for the same hormones that help you bounce back from stress are to blame for brain burnout.

Meltdown

The most sensitive region of your brain to a stress meltdown is your hippocampus, because it has a particularly high number of receptors that are sensitive to the effects of stress hormones, in particular cortisol. Hippocampal meltdown, or atrophy, as it is more correctly termed, is as you would expect a generally bad thing.

Your hippocampus is vital to your ability to control your food intake, learn, remember and place emotional events in context. Also, the hippocampus regulates the systemic stress response including the fight-flight response (the sympathetic nervous system) and your adrenals (the hypothalamic-pituitary-adrenal axis). So losing your hippocampus would spell losing control over your appetite, emotions and ability to handle stress.

Hippocampal atrophy may also underlie adrenal burnout, anxiety, insomnia, depression, cognitive decline, and dementia and Alzheimer's disease. These conditions have long been associated with chronic stress, and recently it has been found that they develop in a sort of continuum, a progressive state of brain meltdown and dysfunction . Stress can cause anxiety, which in turn precedes insomnia, insomnia gives rise to depression and depression results in cognitive impairment, which is the stepping stone for dementia and Alzheimer's disease. The brain over time burns out.

If you are like most people, you are under constant stress

whether you realise it or not. Financial worries, work stress, demanding relationships or lack of support, repressed emotional trauma and nagging health concerns all take their toll, no matter how well we seem to hold it together. The good news is you can grow back your broken brain.

Signs of hope

One of the first signs of hope was reported over a decade ago when a group of Cushing's syndrome patients grew back their brains. (Cushing's syndrome is a condition characterised by very high levels of the stress hormone cortisol and is an archetypical example of chronic stress. Sufferers of this disease get all the symptoms of chronic stress – obesity, heart disease, and depression for example – just much faster). By lowering cortisol levels in these patients it was possible to increase hippocampal volume, that is, the hippocampus repaired and regenerated itself.

It is a myth that you are given a certain number of brain cells at birth and that if you abuse and destroy your quota, by drinking too much in college for example, that you will never get your brain cells back. The truth is that your brain is plastic. In neurology the term "neuroplasticity" refers to the ability of the human brain to change as a result of one's experience, a process that involves changes in your brain structure and the growth of new cells. That's right; your brain has the capacity for regeneration and repair.

Taken together, the understanding that stress can cause degeneration of your hippocampus, and that your brain also has the capacity to repair itself begs the question; how can I grow back a broken brain? This is a relatively new, and unexplored area, but here a few strategies that may help:

1. Free your mind

Meditation has been shown to influence the activity of several brain regions and change concentrations of neurotransmitters; this may explain why there are so many studies suggesting benefit in neurological and stress related diseases, from anxiety to dementia. Regular meditation practice has been associated with increased hippocampal size. Try this simple meditation exercise (**http://tinyurl.com/tfwmeditation**) to increase your brain size.

2. Eat more fat
The reason your brain got so big in the first place may be because of long term (long term being about 2.3 million years!) consumption of an omega-3 fatty acid rich diet. Omega-3 fats are not only a great source of calories for our big, energy hungry brains, they also increase neuroplasticity, they are the ultimate brain food. People who get more omega-3 fats (in particular DHA and EPA) in their diets have bigger brains as a whole and a larger hippocampus. Good sources of these fats are cold water fish, fish oil supplements, omega-3 enriched eggs, game meats and grass fed beef and lamb.

3. Put friends first
Socialising more has been shown to lower stress hormones in humans, and in animal models at least, social isolation damages the hippocampus. Apart from perhaps increasing your brain size, socialising more is also likely to increase your sense of optimism, lower your risk of heart disease and just make you a happier person.

4. Move your body
If there was a drug that could mimic the effects of exercise, 90% of medicine would likely become obsolete overnight. But it's never going to happen. When it comes to the brain, exercise is king; moving regularly has been shown to reverse hippocampal loss, even in the elderly, a benefit that translates to an anti-aging effect on the brain and improved cognitive function.

5. Cut back the cake
Increases in circulating blood glucose that characterise diabetes and insulin resistance are toxic to the brain. This may

explain why people with type 2 diabetes typically have decreased hippocampal volume, and are more prone to depression and dementia. So apart from increasing waist line (which is also associated with a smaller hippocampus), refined foods and simple sugars are shrinking your brain, but maybe that's why we go back for more.

© Ben Brown, 2012. All rights reserved.

Ben Brown, ND, is an Australian-trained naturopath who has maintained a clinical naturopathic practice, worked in research and development, lectured internationally on natural medicine, conducted training courses and authored numerous articles (see www.timeforwellness.org). Benjamin is a consultant to Nutri Ltd: www.nutri.co.uk

Part 4: Practitioner Proficiencies

Chapter 10: The Difference that makes the Difference

It's important in any business to have a way of measuring your progress against your ethos, goals, values and targets.

In business the most common measurement, also used as a benchmark against other businesses in the same industry, is results against targets - normally turnover against costs. A CAM practice is unusual in that we're also wanting to track some "imponderables".

For example, a consistent theme throughout Mark's columns in CAM magazine has been "the difference that makes the difference". His idea is to encourage practitioners to go that extra mile for their clients. "Include within your proposition a service that can't be matched on any level, then this itself defines there is no competition for you", he says."The difference that makes the difference" is the way to achieve truly exceptional results, but it's a little difficult to measure as there are so many factors involved in "going the extra mile".

To get round this, Mark invented "Practitioner Proficiencies", which regular readers of CAM magazine will be familiar with. In his monthly columns he's been explaining how to develop these. What he hasn't really explained until now is that the Practitioner Proficiencies double as a set of measurable quantifiers deemed business critical to the running of a sustainable, successful private CAM practice.

In any other slightly less complicated field of business, Practitioner Proficiencies would be seen as a type of Key Performance Indicators (KPIs). Mark has pioneered the idea of using Practitioner Proficiencies as the CAM industry's very own KPIs. So let's briefly look at what standard KPIs actually are.

• Introducing Key Performance Indicators

KPIs are a set of measures in which a business defines and measures its success against its goals. They are very common and are widely used in both public and private sectors.

In the world of a CAM practitioner, our success is based upon seeing a certain number of clients, so therefore a KPI would be the measurement of how many clients were being seen each month. A lack of clients would be critical to our business and would indicate our success or failure against that KPI. Let's look at some more examples:

- A college may focus its KPIs on intake numbers or graduating students.
- Ford may focus Its KPIs on numbers of cars manufactured during a given period.
- A restaurant may have a KPI that focuses on returning diners.
- An A and E department of a hospital may have a KPI based on waiting times.

Whatever KPIs are selected they must reflect the ethos and goals of that business and be quantifiable, measurable, and key to the success of the business. KPIs are normally long term considerations, although the way they are measured often changes as a business gets nearer to achieving its goals. By the same token, if the business is moving farther away from achieving its goals, KPIs and their measurement may get tougher and become even more focused

• Measuring Key Performance Indicators

If a KPI is going to be of any value there must be a way to accurately define and measure it. It's important each KPI carries a target and is measured regularly.

• **Practitioner Proficiencies**

Mark spent a long time deliberating about what to include as Practitioner Proficiencies. The pay-off was obvious. Assuming he got the KPIs right and he really could measure his business performance against CAM-type goals that are not just about money, then if his business would not only succeed on every level but could be measured on its way against intangibles like whether it was staying true to its values: that was really important, as it is to most CAM practitioners.

These were Mark's initial business goals:

- To offer unequalled client service
- To ensure every client experience was first-class
- To offer clients something they couldn't find anywhere else
- To attract and retain High Value Clients and to obtain Referrals
- To keep up to date with my own skills and knowledge
- To turnover £100k, growing by 20% every year
- To offer a range of training and mentoring services deemed industry-leading by my students and competitors
- To be a leading industry expert and voice in the media
- To create a brand and profile known throughout the UK with Life Practice coaching clinics throughout the UK
- To adhere and embrace the emerging development of regulation within the CAM business
- To ensure my own skills and knowledge and those of my Associates were kept current and up to date
- To offer a range of therapeutic disciplines to my clients,enabling me to work with a different and varied client base, securing my business with a solid foundation of different types of client

He then needed to come up with a set of Key Performance Indicators that embraced the above values, coupled with business income and commercial action plan. He arrived at these:

1. Client complaints
2. Ongoing CPD
3. Achieving a level of weekly activity in the following client areas
    *   New Clients each week
    *   Total clients appointments each week
    *   Client Enquires each week
    *   Referrals each week
4. Achieving the correct business mix of conditions treated each week
5. Compliance and supervision

• The Big 5 KIPs for CAM practitioners

1 Key Performance Indicator = Client Complaints

Business Goal = To offer unequalled client Service.
Quantifiable and Measurable - Yes

How = Target zero client complaints each year

2 Key Performance Indicator = CPD

Business Goal = To ensure skills and knowledge and those of Associates were kept current and up to date
Quantifiable and Measurable - Yes

How = Target for CPD hours per annum

3 Key Performance Indicator = Sales Activity Levels

Business Goal = To attract and retain the right number of High Value Clients and Referrals by achieving a certain number of client appointments and new enquiries each week
Quantifiable and Measurable = Yes

How = Agree actions and manage targets for the activity levels in the areas of focus:Appointments, New Clients, Referrals, Enquiries

4 Key Performance Indicator = Business Mix

Business Goal = To offer a range of therapeutic disciplines to clients enabling work with a different and varied client base securing the business with a solid foundation of different types of client
Quantifiable and Measurable - Yes

How = Market into a client arena to match your skills, interests and qualifications

5 Key Performance Indicator = Compliance and Supervision

Business Goal = To adhere and embrace the emerging development of regulation within CAM

Quantifiable and Measurable = Yes
How = To embrace voluntary self-regulation and appoint a supervisor agreeing a programme of monitoring and supervision, formally reviewed monthly

• The next steps - managing your KPIs

The next step is to have a simple way to monitor KPI results every month and then have an automatic action and follow-through process where KPI targets hadn't been met. There's no point in having a KPI process without including a follow up action as part of the process.

The easiest and most effective way is to use the goal review process called GROW that we have already looked at earlier in the book. At your monthly review, formally review and record your results against your KPI targets and then add respective areas that need attention to a rolling year action plan for the year.

Remember, your KPIs are the business critical measurement of your business goals and actions. They are crucial to the success of any business. Every single KPI carries a target of some sort, as it has to be quantifiable and measurable.

Let's look at targets within each individual KPI.

1. **Complaints** – Set a target of how many complaints are acceptable each year. It is not uncommon to see a zero in here. It's a great idea to have a complaints log in your practice so that any negative feedback or complaint can be logged and investigated. If you have a supervisor, then they would conduct an investigation, otherwise there should be someone in your professional association who handles this if necessary.

2. **CPD** - Targets vary from discipline to discipline. Regulatory requirements always seem to be on the low side, so use that benchmark as a minimum.

3. **Sales activity levels** - All four areas of activity - Enquires, Client Appointments, New clients and Referrals - will carry a target in line with the income and financial needs of your practice. Behind each of these four target areas will be a set of focused actions to ensure the practice achieves this KPI.

4. **Business mix** - Where a practitioner holds qualifications in a number of different disciplines it is common to target weekly or monthly across the disciplines. For example, a nutritional Therapist may also be fully qualified in NLP, Hypnotherapy and Life Coaching.It would be quite normal to see a 25% split in targeting across all four disciplines, monitored every month. This potentially creates more opportunity for income

5. **Compliance and supervision** - In our world of changing regulation and standards, you need a regulatory supervisor. Often two practitioners can

supervise each other. This enables compliance hotspots (Occupational Standards) to be monitored, investigated and formally logged each month and held on file. Targets can be set for certain standards to be agreed within the area of compliance.

• Bringing it all together

Use a basic review form that will enable you to bring together all the information you require for all five KPIs: review every month.Once you have completed your monthly KPI review you add any new actions onto your rolling business action plan, documenting them on the KPI sheet for that respective month and then file the sheet, having it available for inspection if required.

Let's have a look at what a KPI Review might look like.

• Case Study: KPI review

Becky runs a very successful clinic. She is very aware that the success of her clinic is down to her location and word of mouth referrals. She needs 15 clients per week to meet her sales targets, which will in turn deliver her the profit she requires.

One of her key values is first-class service; she knows this produces referrals and she works very hard at going that extra mile for her clients.

Her gross income target is £60,000 a year. She is qualified in Kinesiology, Clinical Hypnotherapy, NLP and Life Coaching. She has targeted for 50% of her clients to come from hypnotherapy, as it is a premium charged therapy, and the rest to come equally between NLP, kinesiology and life coaching. She likes a mixed spread of clients as she finds some disciplines more difficult than others.

Becky operates in a private clinic she rents from her landlord and one of her main interests is keeping her skills and knowledge up to date.

She has set herself a target of completing 100 hours a year of personal CPD and will attend various courses and seminars.

She is very focused on obtaining new clients and looks to close as many of her enquires as she can. To allow for some natural slippage, she targets herself for 5 new enquiries a week and 10 new clients per month. She targets 1 referral per week. She closes around 50% of all her enquiries.

She works with her supervisor and they meet once a month. Her supervisor likes to check two cases each month to give support and her opinion where required. That amounts to a minimum of 4 checks per year in each therapeutic discipline. She uses that opportunity to conduct a KPI review which is documented, filed and any actions taken forward.

This is her completed KPI review sheet for September 2012:

You can see how simple a full KPI review can be using a simple process and form. Set your own KPIs depending on your areas of discipline, but definitely include Complaints, Sales Targets, Activity levels, CPD and Compliance and supervision.

KPI	Month 9 Annual Target	Target	Actual	YTD	Comments	C/F AP
Complaints	0	0	0	0	Maintain current performance	n/a
CPD	100 hours	8.5	5	97	Ahead of target - well done	n/a
Sales Activity Levels						
Enquiries % of plan	240	20	10 50%	115 86%	Actions needed to address	Yes
Client Appts % of plan	640	60	48 80%	456 92%	Actions needed to address	Yes
New Clients % of plan	110	10	15 150%	100 125%	Good results, well done, need now to sustain to drive other activity areas	Yes

Referrals % of plan	48	4	6	40 120%	Good results, well done, need now to sustain to drive other activity areas	Yes
Business mix						
Nutrition	15%	15%	40%	30%	Review action plan in line with current performance	Yes
NLP- Life Coaching	10%	10%	10%	5%	Review action plan in line with current performance	Yes
Hypnotherapy	50%	50%	20%	25%	Review action plan in line with current performance	Yes
Kinesiology	25%	25%	30%	40%	Review action plan in line with current performance	Yes
Compliance & supervision	22 cases	2 cases	2cases	18	On track, no issues to date	n/a

Chapter 11: Regulation

This chapter looks at the regulation of professional practice in healthcare in general and in complementary healthcare in particular. (CAM - Complementary and Alternative Medicine - is used as shorthand throughout when referring to the whole sector). At a time when the public are becoming more aware of their rights and are increasingly willing to complain about care which does not meet their expectations, it is important for you, as a practitioner, to understand the checks and balances that are in place to protect both practitioners and the public. Here we have given free rein to Maggy Wallace, MA, Chair of The Complementary and Natural Healthcare Council, to explain the history behind, and the rationale for, regulation.

I know that the idea of regulation of any sort sits uncomfortably with some practitioners but it is a fact of life and knowing about it will help you to manage your professional practice more efficiently. This is also a good time to be getting up to speed with what is happening, as there are significant changes afoot which are likely to affect you. Boring? - it doesn't have to be. Useful? - without a doubt. Necessary? - absolutely. So do please read on

The overall picture

Just to re-cap in case you're not quite sure who does what.

There are basically two main types of organisations that you need to understand about here, although there may be some overlap of function: *regulatory bodies* and *professional bodies/ associations*.

Regulatory bodies exist primarily in the <u>public interest</u>. They hold public registers which have explicit standards for practitioner entry, maintenance (eg Continuing Professional Development (CPD)) and removal from the register. They often work with professional associations (see below) to improve standards of practice but their main function is to ensure that all those registered meet defined standards of competence and safety and, most importantly, that they can call you to account if a complaint is made against you. Outside CAM the best known regulatory body is probably The General Medical Council (GMC) for doctors. Within CAM, the regulatory body set up in 2008 at the instigation of and with support and funding from the Department of Health is the Complementary and Natural Healthcare Council (CNHC).

Professional Associations /Bodies exist primarily to support their <u>members</u>, to improve standards of professional practice, to offer CPD and to keep their members abreast of changes in practice and healthcare generally. They keep a register of members and there may be some criteria to be met before admission. Their prime focus is their members, who pay a fee to join and receive information and help of various kinds. They also offer support in the event of a complaint being made against one of their own members. Again, outside CAM, probably the best known Professional Association is The British Medical Association (BMA). Within CAM there are various bodies, those which may be for one group of practitioners only, such as The Association of Reflexologists (AoR); or those for different groups such as The Federation of Holistic Therapies (FHT).

Statutory Regulation

Many of the UK healthcare regulatory bodies have been set up as the result of legislation and are therefore known as statutory bodies (ie underpinned by law). The main advantages of statutory regulation are protection of title eg Registered Midwife, and the fact that you cannot practise your profession without being registered. The statutory healthcare bodies are the General Medical Council (GMC), the General Dental Council (GDC), the Nursing and Midwifery Council (NMC), the Health and Care Professions Council (HCPC), The General Osteopaths Council (GOsC); The General Chiropractic Council (GCC); The General Ophthalmic Council (GOC); The General Pharmaceutical Council (GPhC) and the Pharmaceutical Society of Northern Ireland (PSNI). Many of these bodies have been in place for many years - often following lengthy and tortuous negotiations to get effective regulation for their professions. Within CAM, Herbal Medicine and Traditional Chinese Medicine are awaiting statutory regulation with HCPC. (see Fig 1).

However, statutory regulation is expensive (for example, chiropractors pay £800 regsitration fee a year), comparatively inflexible and any changes take a long time and a lot of money to put into place. Partly as a result of these considerations and partly as result of a changing political approach to regulation, statutory regulation is no longer considered to be the favoured option for professional regulation within healthcare, unless the associated risks are considered to warrant such an approach.

Hence we come to voluntary regulation.

Voluntary regulation

Voluntary regulation means that there is no legislation to underpin the regulatory process, although the structures may be very similar to that of a statutory body. Although this has significant advantages with lower costs, speed of change and increased flexibility, it does have two major drawbacks in that such regulation is not a legal requirement for professional practice and professional titles are not protected in law. However, if a voluntary system is robust, has clear visible standards and everyone within the relevant industry and the public know about it, then a voluntary system can be very effective. For example, you would be very unlikely to book a holiday with a company that wasn't approved by ABTA (Association of British Travel Agents), wouldn't you? If a body is ABTA registered you know that in the event of anything going wrong, you have recourse to complaint and resolution. Yet to be ABTA registered is not a requirement of legislation but an agreement of good practice amongst the travel industry.

Voluntary regulation is now being used more widely in healthcare as a result of changing governmental policies and can have many advantages, providing as many people as possible sign up to it and believe in its effectiveness. To understand how this works in healthcare with application to CAM, we need to step aside for a while to look at the background to CAM regulation.

Background to CAM regulation

House of Lords Select Committee Report on Science and Technology

Although there had been a range of *ad hoc* activity – some very good but also some very variable - within CAM in terms of setting standards before 2000, the most significant event to affect the sector and to lead to where we are now, came in November 2000.This was when the House of Lords Select Committee on Science and Technology produced a report on complementary and alternative medicine (HoL 2000). Taking evidence from a wide range of groups and individuals over a period of fifteen months, the wide ranging and influential report was published. The final report organised therapies into groups, as follows:

Group 1 Professionally organised alternative therapies: "*Principal disciplines which claim to have an individual diagnostic approach and are considered the 'big 5' by most of the CAM world"*.

- acupuncture
- chiropractic
- herbal medicine
- homeopathy
- osteopathy

Group 2 Complementary therapies : *"Therapies which are most often used to complement conventional medicine and do not purport to embrace diagnostic skills"*

- Alexander technique
- Aromatherapy
- Bach and other flower remedies
- Body work therapies, including massage
- Counselling stress therapies
- Hypnotherapy
- Meditation
- Reflexology
- Shiatsu
- Healing
- Maharishi Ayurvedic Medicine
- Nutritional medicine
- Yoga

Group 3 Alternative disciplines: *"Those which purport to offer diagnostic information as well as treatments...which are indifferent to the scientific principles of conventional medicine"*

Group 3a – includes long established and traditional systems of healthcare

- anthroposophical medicine
- Ayurvedic Medicine
- Chinese Herbal Medicine
- Eastern Medicine
- Naturopathy
- Traditional Chinese Medicine

Group 3b Other alternative disciplines

"Other alternative disciplines which lack any credible evidence base"

- crystal therapy
- dowsing
- iridology
- kinesiology
- radionics

Recommendations

The full report makes interesting reading. But if you don't have time for that, you do need to know that the Committee's main recommendation in relation to regulation was "that the public interest will best be served by improved regulatory structures of many CAM professions". This recommendation was the main driver for most of the regulatory activity over the next ten years, as follows.

The Prince's Foundation for Integrated Health

Following the House of Lords' Select Committee report, the Prince's Foundation for Integrated Health (PFIH), with monies initially from The King's Fund and then the Department of Health, started work with fifteen disciplines, mainly from Group 2 of the Report, to start the process of consistent standard setting across the groups concerned. A huge amount of time and effort was expended in getting standards into place within the sector. At first, interested disciplines were asked to work on the preparation of standards for profession-specific registers. However, following The Stone Report (PFIH 2005), it was agreed that a different approach would be more appropriate and that it would be in the best interests of the public, the professionals and the industry to set up a Federal

Regulatory Body for the CAM sector as a whole. PFIH's work culminated in a working group which met during 2007 and was chaired by Dame Professor Joan Higgins.

The working group prepared a final report published in 2008 (PFIH 2008) which provided the impetus for the establishment of the independent voluntary regulatory body for complementary healthcare which became known as the Complementary and Natural Healthcare Council (www.cnhc.org.uk).

The Complementary and Natural Healthcare Council

The CNHC Board was appointed in December 2007 and took office in January 2008. A huge amount of work was undertaken in that first year, both to establish the organisation as a company limited by guarantee and in terms of professional standard setting including:

- agreeing CNHC's values, mission and objectives
- agreeing the entry criteria for registration
- preparing all the Fitness to Practise procedures and processes
- finalising the Code of Conduct, Performance and Ethics
- establishing a web site with an on-line register
- advertising, interviewing and appointing committee members
- numerous meetingswith representatives of the various therapies
- undertaking a wide variety of speaking engagementswith various therapy groups
- making contact with a range of key stakeholders both within and outside the profession
- making regular reports to the Department of Health on progress.

The register actually opened in January 2009 with practitioners from massage, followed by those from nutritional therapy. More disciplines gradually came on board over time as they became ready. The Department of Health grant finished, as agreed, in March 2010 and income is now derived from registration fees only. By 2012 practitioners from fourteen different disciplines are eligible to register and there are well over 5000 names on the CNHC register.

Who can register with CNHC?

Practitioners who meet the entry standards can now register in the following disciplines:

- Alexander technique teaching
- Aromatherapy
- Bowen therapy
- Healing
- Hypnotherapy
- Massage therapy
- Microsystems acupuncture
- Naturopathy
- Nutritional Therapy
- Reflexology
- Reiki
- Shiatsu
- Sports therapy
- Yoga therapy

The value of regulation through CNHC

So, why would you want to register? Why would you choose to pay another fee from your hard-earned income, given that you probably also belong to a professional association? Probably the main reason is because such registration confirms that you have met national standards of competence, which clearly sets you apart from those who may only have completed a weekend course. Here are a few other reasons:

Fig 1 The current position (2012) in relation to healthcare regulation

Healthcare Regulation
- setting standards for education, training and professional practice

Statutory regulation (legislative)	Voluntary regulation
General Chiropractic Council (GCC): **chiropractors**	Complementary and Natural Healthcare Council (CNHC):
General Dental Council (GDC): **dentists, dental nurses, dental technicians, clinical dental technicians, dental hygienists, dental therapists and orthodontic therapists**	**Complementary healthcare practitioners in:** *Aromatherapy* *Alexander Technique teaching* *Bowen therapy*
General Medical Council (GMC): **doctors**	*Healing* *Hypnotherapy*
General Optical Council (GOC): **optometrists & dispensing opticians**	*Massage* *Microsystems* *Acupuncture*
General Osteopathic Council (GOsC): **osteopaths**	*Naturopathy* *Nutritional therapy* *Reflexology* *Reiki*
General Pharmaceutical Council (GPhC): **pharmacists**	*Shiatsu* *Sports therapy* *Yoga therapy*
Health and Care Professions Council (HCPC) **art therapists, biomedical scientists ,chiropodists/podiatrists, clinical scientists, dieticians, hearing aid dispensers, occupational therapists, operating department practitioners, orthoptists,paramedics, physiotherapists, practitioner psychologists, prosthetists/ orthotists, radiographers, social workers(from 2012) ,speech and language therapists. ***	*In the process of becoming regulated with* **CNHC:** *Craniosacral therapy* British Acupuncture Council (BAcC): **acupuncturists**
Nursing and Midwifery Council (NMC): **nurses and midwives**	Other professional groups [eg **psychotherapists, counsellors, homeopaths**] by various professional bodies
Traditional Chinese Medicine and Herbal Medicine are awaiting regulation with HCPC	

Government recognition

- CNHC was set up at the instigation of, and with funding and support from, the Department of Health to set and maintain standards in the complementary healthcare sector.

Being on the national register

- CNHC registered practitioners appear on its UK register, which has received over 170,000 searches since the register opened in 2009.

- Registered practitioners are able to include details of their website on their register entry.

Employment advantages

- An increasing range of bodies, such as employers and insurers, are using CNHC registration and the CNHC quality mark as an independent validation of standards. Other healthcare professionals are becoming more likely to suggest when patients are seeking complementary therapies, that they use CNHC registered practitioners.

Private health cash plans

- An increasing number of private health cash plan providers accept CNHC registration as a condition for paying claims.

Public Relations support

- Practitioners from around the UK have been featured in local newspapers, in magazines and on local radio with many seeing an increase in enquiries and clients as a result of using CNHC's PR support materials to publicise their CNHC registration.

Wider influence in the policy arena

- CNHC provides a strong public interest voice for complementary healthcare in the wider policy field.

CNHC and professional associations working together

- The CNHC and professional associations are working together to raise and maintain standards of practice. As with other healthcare professionals, we recommend that practitioners should be members of a professional association and also register with CNHC.

What next?

One of the problems with issues like regulation is that things are always on the move: just as you get used to one thing, it changes. So, what's new right now? The main change that is likely to affect CNHC relates to another regulatory body (there are so many of them!!). This time it's the Council for Healthcare Regulatory Excellence (CHRE), sometimes called the 'super-regulator'. At the moment CHRE has explicit responsibility in relation to the statutory healthcare regulators (see www.chre.org.uk). However, the Health and Social Care Act (2012) gives the body new powers to accredit registers run by voluntary organisations in health and social care. CHRE is also changing its name to The Professional Standards Authority for Health and Social Care (PSA), so I will use that name from now on. So, what does this mean for CNHC in particular and CAM in general?

Basically, all health and social care regulation is going to come within the remit of the PSA – whether statutory or voluntary. It is likely that unless a complementary healthcare practitioner is registered on an accredited register, employment will become very difficult. As indicated earlier, an increasing number of organisations are requiring CNHC registration already for employment and when, as anticipated, CNHC is accredited by the PSA, this will become even more important. So the CNHC Quality mark will sit alongside the PSA accreditation confirming to the public and other professionals that those on the register have met stringent standards and can be called to account if necessary.

Keep your eyes open to see what else happens.....it is likely to affect you.

So what does this mean for you?

To recap, I hope that you are now convinced that regulation is important for all professionals. It demonstrates that you take your professional status seriously and that you are willing to stand up and be counted by having your name on a public register. This confirms that you have met national standards of competence; that you keep up to date; and that you are willing to be called to account if necessary. Many people have fought very hard over the years to achieve this recognition for complementary health and I am sure that you will want to be one of those who are proud to be registered. It also means that you are contributing significantly to the influence of complementary health on wider health issues. Also the more practitioners who come together as a single voice (under the CNHC) the stronger the CAM sector will become. Also, importantly, the more people who engage in, and contribute to, debate on health policy issues, the greater will be the available choice for consumers.

References

(1) House of Lords *Complementary and Alternative Medicine* 22 November 2000 5th Report HL 121 ISBN 0 10 444200 XHoL Report
(2) Stone, J, 2005. *Development of proposals for a future voluntary regulatory structure for complementary*

healthcare professions. London: The Prince of Wales's Foundation for Integrated Health. London.

(3) PFIH *2008 A Federal Approach to Professional-led Voluntary Regulation for Complementary Healthcare. A Plan for Action.* . The Prince of Wales's Foundation for Integrated Health. London

(4) The Health and Social Care Act 2012

Websites

Council for Healthcare Regulatory Excellence (CHRE) www.chre.org.uk 157-197 Buckingham Palace Road, London SW1W 9SP, 020 7389 8030,
Fax: 020 7389 8040.

Complementary and Natural Healthcare Council (CNHC) www.cnhc.org.uk 83, Victoria Street, London SW1H 0HW, 020 178 2196.

Part 5: Your Future – Putting it all Together

Chapter 12

10 Steps to a Better Business

Mike Ash

Mike Ash is one of Britain's best-known and most highly respected practitioners and educators, who with colleague Antony Haynes runs regular Profitable Practice Seminars. He is CAM magazine's Contributing Editor. Here he gives 10 practical suggestions for running your business – based on his 25 years in practice .

1. Manage your money

More than ever, your finances need to be managed in a productive way. Take the time to consider what return on investment you are likely to see. Does the testing machine you are looking at really add value, or would you be better spending the money on a journal subscription or more CPD attendances. Maybe a practice management seminar!

People respond to people and what defines complementary and alternative medicine is the consensus of care that emerges from a consultation in which both parties are willing to support each other's objectives. Data is a very important part of this, but is really valued when contextually used, as opposed to being squeezed into the consult to pay for the cost of the machine.

Advertising is normally difficult to justify for a small practice, but a good website is a must. These can be set up for just a few pounds these days – content should be accurate, readable, and understandable and reflect your skill sets. Because of the situation with the ASA [see chapter 5], claims need to carefully reviewed.

2. Learn to sell

Our clinical skills, when well-honed, are a perfect example of mutual selling; the patient reveals or sells us their problems and we sell these back to them as a review of their story with associated proposals/treatments that can be very challenging to implement.

Lifestyle changes are complex and fraught with difficulties, so having a clear understanding of what the patient can and cannot achieve, moulding those changes to remain effective and achievable is all part of the "selling" of lifestyle medicine. Remember that how you are, how you act, function, appear and address their concerns give off powerful messages. If you are timid, or overwhelmed by the situation, or try to bluff your way through a complicated conversation, it will be seen as a reason not to apply your recommendations.

3. Cut out wasteful time

Once you start to see more patients, the first thing is to learn how to avoid over-supply of information. Create standard letter and email templates, ensure that your terms of engagement are clear and then stick to them. This is cheaper than hiring a member of staff or colleague. Only when these areas have been fully utilised is it a good idea to think about expanding the number of practitioners in your consulting domain.

4. You are not part of the NHS

Remember that despite the fact we have been brought up on the notion that in the UK healthcare is free at the point of entry – it is not – you are not in private practice to compete with the "free" NHS. You need to make money to survive.

Get over, suitably fast, the fear of money and of charging, otherwise you will become a part of our society that needs to rely on the social support structure you are trying to contribute to by paying tax on profit, rather than getting benefits because you are unable to make your practice survive financially.

Realise that the only purpose your business has is to make money. Save the world once you've made some. In the meantime, leave "social enterprises" to charities and governments.

5. Think about your finances
Clinical life is also business life – there is no conflict in this relationship, unless the recommendations you make for tests and products are driven by profit motive rather than clinical need. Stick to the ethical application of expert knowledge and professional supplements – see results and make a living, then everyone remains happy.

Find an accountant, join the Federation of Small Businesses, attend workshops on self-promotion, borrow as little as you need and be sure you have a sensible repayment plan. Put as much effort into the management of the financials as you do into your on-going education for just 1 day per month and you will really make an economic difference to your clinical success.

6. Exploit niches
Avoid the big wide gate and overly saturated markets and concentrate on the niche, then look at your competitors in your niche market to get an idea of where you're going to find customers. A successful practice is the one that does things better than its competitors. So analyse the marketplace and improve on it. Become expert in one or two dominant areas and then use this skill to migrate into other sectors. Link up with colleagues who have expertise in allied but different fields and create referral systems.

7. Really care for your clients/patients

Your business plan should be five words long: "Get and keep more customers!"

Without customers you haven't got a business, and by customers, I mean people who spend money. Look after your client/patient list. Create a good database of clients/patients and prospects. Your database is a precious resource, so ensure you look after it through regular email and telephone contact with clients, former clients and prospective clients. Let them know you're thinking of them.

Remember that when you are seeing someone the focus is on them; they do not want to hear a 2-hour lecture on how they got to where they are – they want a professional guide and shared support to get out of the situation they are in. Focus and deliver.

8. Be realistic

Give yourself time to build up your business and don't expect to become profitable overnight. Knowing it's likely to take a long time keeps you at a realistic level. The vast majority of people overestimate what they can achieve in a year, and massively underestimate what they can achieve in a decade. Just make sure you celebrate the small victories along the way to keep yourself motivated.

9. Get education

Read CAM, subscribe to journals (don't just read soft articles in consumer magazines) or visit websites such as www.nleducation.co.uk every week:review the articles and make notes; you have a responsibility to keep up with changing data and opinion, do not simply stop when you qualify and then rely on information that is more than 1-2 years old.

For your business skills, everything you ever wanted to know is contained in a book somewhere, so read everything you can about people who have started businesses from nothing — preferably biographies and autobiographies. You'll find everything you need to know is within those pages. Use what you learn to improve your business acumen daily. Find and read short tips and strategies, you are not simply a CAM practitioner, you are also a self-employed business person – get used to it.

10. Believe in yourself

Self-belief is a practitioner's most precious commodity. If you don't believe in yourself, then you can't expect customers to. Procrastination is the enemy of all self-employed people.

In a nutshell, you procrastinate when you put off things that you should be focusing on right now, usually in favour of doing something that is more enjoyable or that you're more comfortable doing.

Procrastination is independent of need for achievement, energy, or self-esteem. In other words, you may be a procrastinator even if you're confident in your own abilities, energetic, and enjoy achieving things. But failing to make a decision is frequently worse than making no decision at all.

Organised people manage to fend off the temptation to procrastinate, because they will have things like prioritised to-do lists and schedules which emphasise how important a piece of work is, and identify precisely when it's due. They'll also have planned how long a task will take to do, and will have worked back from that point to identify when they need to get started in order to avoid it being late. Organised people are also better placed to avoid procrastination, because they know how to break the work down into manageable "next steps".

- Keep a To-Do list so that you can't "conveniently" forget about unpleasant or overwhelming tasks.

- Use an Urgent/Important Matrix to help prioritise your to-do list so that you can't try to kid yourself that it would be acceptable to put off doing something on the grounds that it's unimportant, or that you have many urgent things which ought to be done first when, in reality, you're procrastinating.
- Become a master of scheduling and project planning, so that you know when to start those all-important projects.
- Set yourself time-bound goals: that way, you'll have no time for procrastination!
- Focus on one task at a time.

If you're putting off starting a project because you find it overwhelming, you need to take a different approach. Here are some tips:

- Break the project into a set of smaller, more manageable tasks. You may find it helpful to create an action plan.
- Start with some quick, small tasks if you can, even if these aren't the logical first actions. You'll feel that you're achieving things, and so perhaps the whole project won't be so overwhelming after all.

If you're procrastinating because you find the task unpleasant:

- Many procrastinators overestimate the unpleasant-ness of a task. So give it a try! You may find that it's not as bad as you thought!
- Hold the unpleasant consequences of **not** doing the work at the front of your mind.
- Reward yourself for doing the task.

Michael Ash, BSc (Hons), DO, ND, F DipION, is the managing director of Nutri-Link Ltd, editor of the clinical education website www.nleducation.co.uk and Contributing Editor to CAM magazine, in which his writing regularly appears. He is an Osteopath, Naturopath and Clinical Nutritionist with more than 25 years experience founding and then running a large, successful integrated medicine clinic. In addition he is a researcher and lecturer as well as an entrepreneur focused on health related business development.

Taking Your Practice To Market

Monica Black

Monica Black is a Clinical Hypnotherapist and NLP practitioner who has set new standards for winning positive media exposure and positioning herself as the "go to" expert. She's an inspiration to many CAM practitioners and someone we could all do well to model.

CONGRATULATIONS!!!After many months of hard studying, dedication, case studies plus much more you are now a qualified therapist.Yippee!!

But wait - hang on a minute. After the euphoria of qualifying, 10 to 1 you're thinking (I know I did) what the heck do I do now?How do I get going?Where do I find my clients? How can my future clients find me? Etc, etc, etc. No need to panic. The best place to start is of course at the beginning. Ask yourself this question "When I need to look for something, where do I go to, to find it?"Almost instinctively you log into Google without a second thought and do a search to find what YOU want. And what pops up? All the websites and details of what you're looking for are staring back at you from your computer screen and beckoning out to you -"choose me, choose me, choose me".

1. You've GOT to have a website

So there's your answer. You need to have a website presence. But you may think, why? You're a therapist after all, not a commercial organization, and you just want to practise your new-found skills and craft, and the thought of putting together a site is tiresome; it's going to be time-consuming, expensive, and then there's the upkeep and updating of it. Actually, a website is an exceptionally inexpensive tool that helps both you and your clients.

You see, we're in the middle of a full-blown Internet revolution and if you don't have a web presence the chances are you'll be missing out on a prospective clientele to those therapists who do. With a site you'll be taken more seriously - a real professional contender – and to your prospective clients your website reflects how successful you are!!

First of all you'll need to get a domain name and this should reflect what kind of a therapist you are. What are you going to be calling yourself /your practice. The name you choose should be easily remembered, strong and durable. You're going to have it for a long time. Something to think about is where you live and work. Let's say you're a reflexologist who lives/works in Brighton – you could call yourself Brighton Reflexology. This gives the impression that you are THE reflexologist for the Brighton area. Or let's say as another example your practice is the north-west part of a city; you could call yourself North West or NW Reflexology. A Kinesiologist from Kent could call themselves Kent Kinesiology. Get the picture? I practise in the Hampstead of London, so I've called myself Hampstead Hypnotherapy. Which means when someone is doing a Google search for a Hypnotherapist in Hampstead my site is one of the first to pop up.

Some of you maybe skilled in putting together your own site, others will prefer to have someone do it for you. However it should be penned by you using your own words, after all only you have in-depth knowledge of what you do and have to offer. Your site will be the first port of call that prospective clients find you.

It's a good idea before you start to research the sites of other therapists in your field so you can get an idea of what's out there, and by seeing what is out there you will begin to formulate on your own how you'd like yours look. Start with the basics and KIS - Keep it SimpleYour site should be representative of who YOU ARE, what YOU DO, what YOU OFFER,where YOU PRACTICE, and how YOU CAN BE CONTACTED and EASY to NAVIGATE- in order that your prospective clients can find the relevant information they need – if navigation is not simple they will, as sure as eggs are eggs, lose patience and more importantly you'll lose business!!

2. How much should you charge your clients?

Now you've got your web site organised you're on your way. Or are you? Not quite. You see the next step in getting up and running and before you can even treat anyone, you need to ask yourself a very important question. "How much should I charge my clients?"

There are many factors to take into consideration as to how you price yourself. Location plays a huge role in determining your charges. If you practise in an area with a higher standard of living, your rates will be higher than if you practise in an area with a lower income bracket.

To determine what other therapists in your discipline and area are charging you will need to do some practical research. Google and local media outlets such as the local newspapers, magazines, and Yellow Pages etc are your best bet. You may very well also discover some therapists advertise their rates while others won't be so transparent. In such cases, telephone and ask about their session costs and length.

Once you are happy with your research, price yourself accordingly. However, be realistic. If you find a practitioner who has many years of experience you can be sure they are charging more than a newly qualified therapist. So price yourself according to your skillset and experience. (You can always increase your costs after a couple of months, once you've gained confidence in your abilities and are building a client/patient base.)

Are you practising out of a clinic and renting a room there, or are you practising out of your home?

Should you decide to go down the clinic route you need to be aware there are 2 different charging methods. They will either charge a percentage of your hourly rate - and this can be anything from 10% to 50% - or they will charge an hourly room rent. All other costs – such as lighting, heating, air-conditioning, couches, towels, gowns (if required), laundry, receptionist, payment taking, appointment making, patient referral etc will be included in the room rental charge.

To make things a bit more complicated, straight room rental can be broken down into another 2 different methods. Usually a therapist is asked to take a "block booking". This means that you are committed to a regular time slot on a day or days of your choice. Say you decide to have a 4-hour block on Tuesdays and Thursdays. This means you will pay for these 8 hours whether you work or not. You pay when you take a vacation, are sick or, as can unfortunately happen on occasions, when you have no one booked in.

The upside, for both you and your clients, is that it is regular, which means both you and your clients can plan your diaries accordingly. Regular clients like standing appointments.

Clinics will also offer "ad hoc'" hours. Ad hoc hours are when you book your room on an "as and when needed" basis. Ad hoc hourly rates are generally more expensive than a block rate. You might also choose to have a mixture of both. The downside to ad hoc hours is 1) it's more expensive; 2) the time slot you need might not be available. The upside is you are not committed to a room rental charge when you are not working!!

In London rents vary from £11 to £20+ per hour. So let's say you charge £80 per hour and your room rent is £20, then your net income per hour is £60. On top of that you have your extra overheads, such as your marketing material, leaflets, brochures, name cards, travelling costs, equipment if needed, in your modality, as well as that horrid word "tax". So you need to ask yourself is that amount of income per hour acceptable, do-able and workable for you?

Remember you are a business not a charity – no matter how much you'd like to be! Most therapists don't realise this and I've found that many therapists think that they are "not in it for the money". Wrong. You've invested your time and money to train to a high standard, and not only do you need to see a return on your training, but you need to pay the mortgage!

Don't underestimate your ability even though you are newly qualified and most likely think or feel that by charging lower than the norm you'll get more clients and build your business that way. Wrong again. You will find you will need to work longer hours to meet your target income and eventually get burn out. You will become disillusioned with your craft and may very well quit it. The knock-on effect of that is your self-esteem and confidence will take a knocking!. You see,people will pay for what is important to them and more often than not when they know the average hourly cost of their treatment is "x" and you are charging less, they'll will instinctively feel you're not any good! So contrary to your belief that you will get more clients by billing less you will in fact get fewer clients then if you bill that bit more and according to the industry standard.

The home practice

Many people have the luxury of having a home with a room that can be turned into a therapy room. What you may think at first is that because you are working out of your home you can bill less because you won't have a clinic room rental. However you should take into account that you are in fact "renting" out your own room to yourself. You have to equip that room with the tools of your craft. Maybe a couch, towels, oils, gowns if you are an osteopath, physio or chiropractor, or chairs and everything and anything that you'll need to practise professionally and that is normally provided to the therapist working out of a clinic. The only advantage I can see by working out of your home is that you do not have any travelling nor travelling costs.

It is also lonely working by yourself and I find that working out of a clinic I have the camaraderie of other like-minded professionals and our modalities quite often dovetail into each other so we have a free, therapist to therapist referral system. And I will always have that Christmas party to go to which I wouldn't have if I worked alone!

Your own clinic

You may decide you'd like to find suitable premises and establish your very own clinic. If you are a newly qualified practitioner this is not such a good idea. Yes of course having your own clinic is something many of you will aspire to - and you should go for it, but if that is the case I strongly urge you to work out of an already established clinic for a couple of years, gain experience in your modality, build up a client base and learn the multi-faceted intricacies of what it takes to run a successful professional holistic CAM clinic.

3. How to become a media expert

The first step to becoming a media expert is for you to realise that you will have to share your expertise and speak up on it. You and you alone have that gift to speak passionately about what you do and love. So here are a few pointers as to how to position yourself. You should know that having a media presence is a great way of expanding your profile and business locally, which in turn can then even lead to a national presence.

Contact local media outlets

First of all contact your local newspaper. Many areas also produce a localised free glossy magazine. Find out who the local reporters and journalists and even editors are in your area and build up a relationship with them. The Health and Lifestyle journalists would be the most appropriate, because they would be more interested in you and your expertise.

You might also think to offer them a free treatment in return for you either writing an article in their publication or having them write about you. This will help you in being recognised as an expert in your field, which can then filter through to the national press. If your area happens to have a local radio station or tv channel, contact them. Find out when they might be doing a report or section on health, but more precisely on your modality, and offer to come along and speak. Offering free treatments to the relevant person handling the programme or article is a great foot in the door.

When the smoking ban was introduced a number of years ago I contacted a local BBC radio station because I discovered they were dedicating a whole Sunday morning programme to the topic. I offered to come and speak and also treat someone of their choice to stop smoking. On the day of the programme I was first of all interviewed about hypnotherapy in general, how it worked, what it could be used for and why it was a very successful stop smoking tool. I was then introduced on air to a person who wanted to stop smoking. She was also interviewed. After the interviews we went off to a private room in order for me to treat her. Once we had finished the session – which took one hour - we went back to the studio and were both interviewed again. Off the back of this one programme my Stop Smoking treatment business exploded.

So find a topical subject you can link your expertise to and in a concise and precise way, pitch yourself as the expert in this field. Remember to make sure you present yourself and what you have to offer as being different to your competitors.

As I said keep it concise, precise and simple (KIS) – in other words if you were on one of the Lifestyle daily tv programmes, what would the strap under your name say?

Start a blog

Write about your expertise and focus on your particular "thing". Develop a relevant discussion and inspire your readers. Perhaps if you're working out of a clinic or even a health club/gym ask if you can post articles on their web site.

Set up a Twitter or Facebook account

With these two social media outlets you'll start a community and network of people who are interested in the same issues you treat. Ask everyone on your mailing list (past clients/patients) to "like" or "Follow" you. Word soon gets around and your name and what you do will grow bigger and bigger by the day.

There is an organization called "Find a TV expert". Get onto their books.Their annual joining cost used to be £100, which is quite a reasonable investment when you think of how your name and practice will grow because of this. They will put you forward for radio and tv programmes looking to do something in your field. However if you wish you can contact the tv stations yourself and put yourself forward. There are also many PR websites out there looking for experts. You could think about posting your very own press release with your contact details. This will then enable journalists and other media enquiries and outlets to contact you.

Most professional governing bodies are occasionally approached by various media outlets. Put yourself on their books as willing to be approached by whoever is looking for an "expert opinion".

Offer to give free talks in your community and to local businesses. As an example you could approach the local WI and offer to give a talk on, let's say, stress and how your particular protocol can help. Word will soon get around and you'll become the local "guru" for the treatment of stress!

Contact charities and offer to talk to them. Maybe your local library has a community educational department. I know a lot of the larger libraries run programmes on complementary and alternative therapy treatments. Put yourself on their books and offer yourself to come and give a talk there on your specialist subject.Maybe you could even organize the whole event.

Find your "hook" - work on it and be persistent, because you deserve to be heard and to be able to share your knowledge and expertise with those people who will benefit most from it. Remember YOU ARE THE EXPERT.

Yes, it is a daunting task to put yourself out there, especially if you are not used to it and have done nothing like this before, but just remember why you are going down this route; why you want to share your expertise in your chosen discipline; how passionate you are about your discipline; and get out there andtell those people all about the benefits of what you do. As Susan Jeffers said: Feel the Fear and Do it Anyway!

4. Joint Ventures

Another excellent way to establish your name and get yourself out there and grow your practice is to form one or more "*Joint Ventures*".

You can form a therapeutical Joint Venture with another professional practitioner whereby you can offer your special expertise to work alongside each other. As an example, a therapist specialising in Fears and Phobias – hypnotherapy/ NLP practitioners in particular - could approach dental practices. Dentists generally have a large proportion of their patients who suffer from dental anxiety. When a dentist is able to offer the patient a way to overcome their fear/phobia/ anxiety thereby enabling them to receive the necessary dental treatment, it enhances the dentists' practice and grows yours.

You and the dentist will need to work out a programme which suits the dentist, you and the patient.

Another 'joint venture' you could think about would be to aligning yourself with your local medical practice. In this day and age our nation is becoming more and more overweight, obese and diabetic and then you have all the knock-on ailments resulting from these conditions (painful knees, bad backs, poor skin, breathlessness, stress, anxiety, as a token sample), Then there are eating disorders such as bulimia and anorexia which need a more specialised approach. A nutritional therapist, physiotherapist, osteopath, massage therapist, podiatrist, sports educationalist, acupuncturist as an example would be ideal partners for the doctor. Why? Because unfortunately our doctors just don't have the time to dedicate and educate their patients with a healthy eating and living plans, whereas these therapists have the expertise to do exactly that.

I feel a good upmarket gym makes an excellent partner. The people you can work alongside would be the personal trainers and you could enhance their spa area also. You could periodically offer to give talks on your specialist subject.

Just have courage to think outside the box and JUST DO IT - I KNOW YOU CAN! You'll be surprised that you'll have great fun doing it.

Monica Black, Master Clinical Hypnotherapist, Master NLP Practitioner, Coach and EFT Practitioner, Hampstead, London:www.hampsteadhypnotherapy.com

Resources

Stay in touch with us

Follow the book on Facebook and please leave your feedback. We love feedback! We're already preparing the second edition, so tell us what extras you'd like to see in it.

Reach Mark Shields via www.lifepractice.co.uk, phone 01462 431 112, Twitter:LifePracticeUK
You can read Mark's CAM Coach column every month in CAM magazine, and look out for news of CAM Coach workshops.

Simon Martin is the editor of CAM, the monthly magazine for practitioners of complementary and alternative medicine: www.cam-mag.com
Contact Simon at simon@metabolicbalancecolorado.com

CMA

The Complementary Medical Association is "a non-profit organisation dedicated to promoting the very highest standards of complementary medicine and natural healthcare". CMA president Jayney Goddard runs regular practice management, marketing and business skills courses for new and established practitioners:www. the-cma.org.uk

Insurance

The Holistic Insurance Company: **0845 222236**, www. holisticinsurance.co.uk

Setting up

www.businesslink.gov.uk
www.companieshouse.gov.uk

"Working for yourself: An Entrepreneur's guide to the basics" by Jonathan Reuvid (Kogan page, 2009).

Federation of Small Businesses – "non-profit making and non-party political" also " the UK's largest campaigning pressure group promoting and protecting the interests of the self-employed and owners of small firms. Formed in 1974, it now has 200,000 members across 33 regions and 194 branches":www.fsb.org.uk

Practice management software
eHealth Practice Management Software: http://ehealth practice.co.uk

PPM Software Ltd, 01992 655940, www.ppmsoftware.com

Websites and website design
www.webhealer.net
www.soulbat.co.uk (Bob Melrose)
www.thetoppageguru.com (Graham Collingwood)
www.google.com/analytics/

Email and newsletter marketing and management
Constant Contact: www.constantcontact.com, 866 876 8464

WordPress: http://wordpress.org
Example of an e-newsletter plug-in for WordPress: http://wordpress.org/extend/plugins/newsletter

Michael Katz: **www.enewslettersystem.com**

Writing and editing
Dawn Josephson, the Master Writing Coach™: www.masterwritingcoach.com

Credit cards
CardSave: http://www.cardsave.net/0800 058 8200

NLP
The basic story of NLP: http://en.wikipedia.org/wiki/ Neuro-linguistic_programming

One of our favourite books on NLP gives you a presupposition a day to work with: "NLP in 21 Days", by Harry Alder and Beryl Heather (Piatkus Books, 2000).

Body language
Handy reference book: "Collins Gem Body Language: How to Understand the Unspoken Language of Your Body" (HarperCollins 2005).

You may also enjoy: "What Every Body is Saying: an ex-FBI Agent's Guide to Speed-Reading People", Joe Navarro with Marvin Kartlins, PhD (HarperCollins, 2008).

Practice management seminars
Profitable Practice seminars: highly recommended. Antony Haynes and Mike Ash explain and teach "proven strategies to make your practice an unqualified success".Usually limited to 25 practitioners, and you have to be seeing at least 10 patients a month: www.nleducation. co.uk, 08450 750 402.

OUR CONTRIBUTORS

Many thanks to:

Michael Ash, BSc (Hons), DO, ND, F DipION, managing director of Nutri-Link Ltd, and editor of the clinical education website www.nleducation.co.uk. He is an Osteopath, Naturopath and Clinical Nutritionist with more than 25 years' experience founding and then running a large, successful integrated medicine clinic. In addition he is a researcher and lecturerand is CAM magazine's Contributing Editor: www.nleducation.co.uk

Monica Black, Master Clinical Hypnotherapist, Master NLP Practitioner,

Coach and EFT Practitioner, Hampstead, London: www. hampsteadhypnotherapy.com

Ben Brown, ND, is an Australian-trained naturopath who has maintained a clinical naturopathic practice, worked in research and development, lectured internationally on natural medicine, conducted training courses and authored numerous articles (see www.timeforwellness.org). Benjamin is a consultant to Nutri Ltd: www.nutri.co.uk

Julie Thompson Crawley: www.bedford-hypnosis-nlp. co.uk

Melanie Firth, Wellbeing Coach: www.lifepracticebrighton.co.uk

Jayney Goddard, Lic LCCH, Dip ACH, FRSPH, President, Complementary Medical Association: www.the-cma.org.uk

Antony Haynes, BA (Hons), Dip ION, mBANT, is Head of Technical Services and cofounder of Nutri-Link, author of " The Insulin Factor" and "The Food Intolerance Bible": www.nleducation.co.uk

Penny Homer, Social Media expert, Sales Operations Manager and Social Media coordinator, Edition Peters Group: homerpenny@gmail.com

Dawn Josephson, the Master Writing Coach™: www.masterwritingcoach.com

Michael Katz, founder and Chief Penguin at Blue Penguin Development (http://bluepenguindevelopment.com), developer of the ace newsletter marketing course: www.enewslettersystem.com

Kate Neil, MSc (Nutritional Medicine), mBANT, NTCC, CNHC, managing director of the Centre for Nutrition Education and Lifestyle Management: www.cnelm.co.uk

Rebecca Smith, Systematic Kinesiologist, Hypnotherapist, NLP Master Practitioner, Proprietor of the Newport Complementary Health Clinic, Newport, Shropshire: www.newportcomplementaryhealthclinic.co.uk

Maggy Wallace, MA, Chair of the The Complementary and Natural Healthcare Council: www.cnhc.org.uk

Front cover design: Hannah Wade, Target Publishing Ltd.

Lightning Source UK Ltd.
Milton Keynes UK
UKOW030444231112

202625UK00001B/36/P